Amazing
Tractors
Facts and Trivia

Amazing Tractors

Facts and Trivia

An illustrated treasury of curiosities, anecdotes, myths, feats of engineering, and unbelievable facts for fans of farm tractors everywhere

Peter Henshaw

CHARTWELL
BOOKS, INC.

A QUARTO BOOK

Published in 2010 by
Chartwell Books, Inc.
A division of Book Sales, Inc.
276 Fifth Avenue, Suite 206
New York, New York 10001
USA

Reprinted 2012

ISBN 13: 978-0-7858-2606-4
ISBN-10: 0-7858-2606-8
QUAR.TFTR

Conceived and designed by
Quarto Publishing plc
The Old Brewery
6 Blundell Street
London N7 9BH

Produced by the Elephant
Book Company Ltd

Commissioning editors:
Will Steeds, Laura Ward
Designer: Mark Roberts,
"talkingdesign"
Project manager: Chris Stone
Picture researcher: Sarah Bell
Copy editor: Karen Stein

Art director: Caroline Guest
Creative director:
Moira Clinch
Publisher: Paul Carslake

Manufactured in Hong Kong
by Modern Age Repro
House Ltd.
Printed in China by
Midas Printing
International Ltd.

Contents

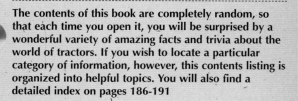

The contents of this book are completely random, so
that each time you open it, you will be surprised by a
wonderful variety of amazing facts and trivia about the
world of tractors. If you wish to locate a particular
category of information, however, this contents listing is
organized into helpful topics. You will also find a
detailed index on pages 186-191

Introduction 6

SPORT

✪ Combine cross 17 ✪ Tractor cross 68 ✪ Tractor racing 92 ✪ Tractor pulling 102, 167 & 181

SPECIALIZED TRACTORS

✪ Corn picker 16 ✪ Forestry 28 ✪ Road roller 29 ✪ Six-wheelers 32 ✪ Snow tractors 39 ✪ Crawlers 46 ✪ Vineyard 47 ✪ Turf 54 ✪ Bidirectional 56 ✪ Orchard 57 ✪ Tractor-trucks 62–63 ✪ Snow blowers 65 ✪ Tricycles 70 ✪ Road hauling 87 ✪ Rotapeds 91 ✪ Mowing 93 ✪ Lifeboat launchers 98 ✪ Tilting tractors 101 & 137 ✪ Rail tractors 105 ✪ High-speed tractors 106–109 ✪ Tandems 110 ✪ Mini-crawlers 127 ✪ Half-tracks 130 ✪ Garden tractors 131 ✪ Wheelchair- compatible 140 ✪ Systems tractors 144 ✪ Industrial 145

HISTORICAL TRACTORS

MILESTONES

CABS

EQUIPMENT

GENERAL TRIVIA

INTRODUCTION

Tractors are amazing—you must know that already, or you wouldn't be reading this book. Just how amazing will be revealed as you turn the pages.

Who was Old Abe, and what is a Mobius Band? Which is better—wheels, or rubber tracks? You'll find the world's first tractor in here, the fastest and the most powerful. Learn how the Soviet Union loved its Fordsons, and why Henry Ford wasn't allowed to call his own tractor a "Ford."

There are tractor stunts, racing, and pulling—why did an Austrian drive a tractor over 4 miles (6.5 km) on two wheels? Did you know that some folk race combine harvesters as well? Well they do, and the rules are revealed here. See how a modern tractor is built, and find out why Allis-Chalmers were painted bright orange for years.

Ferrari, Porsche, and Lamborghini—all of them well-known sports car manufacturers, but the same badges have appeared on tractors. A Ferrari that can plow a field, now there's a thought. Snoopy wasn't just a cartoon dog, and 1930s art deco elegance influenced tractor styling. Lovers of music and literature will discover tractor themes they never knew existed.

There's practical stuff here too—how to plow a field, how to look after a three-point linkage and maintain a tractor, plus driving tips. How to calculate the ideal amount of wheel slip, and ballast a tractor properly.

Think of AMAZING TRACTOR FACTS AND TRIVIA as a sort of pick 'n' mix. Use the contents at the front of the book, or the index at the back, or just dip into it and see what you find. If it's anything like my experience in writing it, you'll have fun.

Peter Henshaw

THE POLISH TRACTOR

Poland isn't known as one of the world's foremost tractor makers, but it has built them for years. Ursus was set up back in 1893 to make industrial equipment, but quickly diversified into internal combustion engines. It made tractors in limited numbers during the 1920s, but didn't get into serious production until after World War II, with a copy of the Lanz Bulldog. In fact Ursus survived by borrowing technology from others. Through the 1960s it was partly dependent on Czech tractor maker Zetor, and from the 1970s built Massey-Fergusons under license.

This tractor speaks fluent Polish.

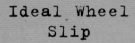
WHAT DOES THAT MEAN?

Front-Wheel Assist

A type of four-wheel drive, where the front wheels are smaller than the rear ones. The fronts are geared to run with more speed (usually 1.3 to 1.4 times faster) to make up for their smaller diameter. This also makes steering easier, and it allows the greater degree of front-wheel slip that is needed for efficient running on tilled soil. The term "front-wheel assist" is less commonly used now, with "four-wheel drive" becoming the generic term.

Ideal Wheel Slip

The ideal wheel slip under full power is 10 to 15 percent for two-wheel drive, or 8 to 12 percent for four-wheel drive or front-wheel assist tractors. The farmer achieves this by adding ballast weights front and rear, but it needs to be done right. An over-ballasted tractor will feel sluggish and use more fuel than it should, and it'll also mean less-than-ideal wheel slip, leading to extra strain on the transmission. An under-ballasted tractor will wear the tires out, thanks to excessive wheel slip, which also means it will never deliver full power at the drawbar and it too will waste fuel. So adding ballast and getting the wheel slip right is literally all about finding the right balance.

Wheel slip: it's all about finding the right balance.

Supercharged Screamer

Two-stroke engines and tractors don't often go together, but the Oliver Super 99 was one of the rare exceptions. Back in 1955, this 70 hp machine was the most powerful tractor on the market.

At the time, the conventional means of obtaining more power was by adding a bigger six-cylinder diesel engine—turbocharging wasn't on the tractor scene yet. Oliver didn't have anything suitable, but employees there did some lateral thinking, had a look around, and opted for the General Motors 3-71 two-stroke. Intended for trucks, this was a three-cylinder supercharged diesel, though unlike a conventional two-stroke it had poppet valves to control the incoming and outgoing gases.

A New Sound in Tractors

The GM motor sounded like no other tractor power unit. Although rated at the same 1,675 rpm as Oliver's own diesels, it produced a unique wailing exhaust note and needed to be kept revving to deliver its power. And it transformed Oliver's biggest tractor, offering 40 percent more power than the conventional gasoline-powered 99, not to mention more torque than John Deere's big Model R diesel. The Super 99 was a tractor hot rod.

On the blower—Oliver's two-stroke screamer had a supercharger to boost power.

That's one hot tractor.

TRACTOR KITSCH

Tractor lovers are as vulnerable to kitsch as anyone else. Here's a selection of the tractor-shaped or themed items you can buy:

- Tractor mugs
- Tractor hats
- Tractor T-shirts
- Tractor weather vanes
- Tractor thermometers
- Tractor hats
- Tractor boots
- Tractor house signs
- Tractor models
- Tractor bead charm
- Tractor stamps
- Tractor kitchen towels
- Tractor clocks
- Tractor bedspreads
- Tractor mouse pad
- Tractor screen saver
- Tractor pocket watch
- Tractor pencil
- Tractor dog blanket

Steam Tractors

Before the tractor, steam power was used on farms. John Wilkinson, a farmer and businessman in North Wales, was a pioneer, installing a steam engine to power a threshing machine in 1798.

But the real breakthrough took another forty years—lighter, portable steam engines that could be towed by horses from farm to farm.

Portable Steam Power

Ransomes of Ipswich showed a portable in 1841. Said to equal the power of five horses, it was demonstrated at the Royal Show that year. One special feature was piping waste steam into the chimney, where the steam would ideally drown the sparks that might otherwise ignite the piles of hay!

A decade later, there were eight thousand portables on British farms. American manufacturers soon followed, and in the early 1900s J. I. Case was one of the world's biggest steam-engine makers. Meanwhile, the steam traction engine had taken over from portables, but it was heavy, expensive, and needed skilled hands to raise steam and operate—leading the way for the development of the lighter, gasoline-powered tractor.

Torque

WHAT DOES THAT MEAN?

Torque is one type of measurement of engine output. Power is a measure of the rate at which work is done, but torque is quite simply how hard the engine can twist a shaft, which is critical to a hard-working tractor. Tractor torque characteristics are carefully designed to allow a high turning effort at relatively low engine speeds.

Those big steamers did a good day's work—the onlookers didn't.

Ergonomic Cabs

Here are the main controls/warning systems in a modern tractor cab:

- ☆ Steering wheel (tiltable)
- ☆ Throttle (foot pedal and hand lever)
- ☆ Clutch
- ☆ Brakes (two pedals)
- ☆ Hydraulics controls
- ☆ Linkage controls
- ☆ Spool valve controls
- ☆ Power takeoff controls
- ☆ Gauges
- ☆ Speedometer/ tachometer
- ☆ Hour meter
- ☆ Voltmeter
- ☆ Fuel level
- ☆ Engine oil pressure
- ☆ Water temperature
- ☆ Digital Monitor
- ☆ Hydraulic flow settings
- ☆ Power usage
- ☆ Wheel slip
- ☆ Fuel consumption
- ☆ Distance traveled
- ☆ Acres (or hectares) covered

Why go home when the cab is this comfy?

Portable Wheat Silo

Portable wheat silos are a handy idea and are most often seen in the big wheat fields of the American Midwest. A silo gives the tractor and trailer or combine somewhere to store grain until a truck arrives to haul it away. Also useful if the main grain store is too far away for a tractor-trailer combination—they'll do it, but slowly.

TOP TIPS

When driving downhill, select low gear and use engine braking to slow the tractor.

Have wheat silo, will travel.

Two wheels good, four wheels dull.

Johann Redl:
Tractor Stunt Driver

Not many people can claim to be tractor stunt drivers, but in the 1990s Johann Redl could. The Austrian worked in carpentry and insurance before being inspired by the American Hell Drivers to become a full-time stunt driver.

His first stunt on a tractor involved driving a Steyr on two wheels for almost 1.8 miles (3 km), in 1991. That was on a closed road, but six years later he tried again on a race track, and this time managed 4.7 miles (7.5 km). And how do you get a tractor up on two wheels? Redl made a special ramp which he would drive up with the offside wheels only, at 18 mph (30 kph)—when the ramp ended, the tractor was left tilting, and some judicious steering would keep it there.

"I'm Alive"

His most dangerous tractor stunt was to suspend a 58 hp Lindner by ropes from a high bridge in the Austrian Tyrol. He then used the tractor's own power to pull itself up the ropes, via pulleys bolted to the wheel rims, which took twenty minutes. At the top, 623 feet (190 m) above the ground, he selected reverse, and the tractor slowly lowered itself back to earth. With feet back on terra firma, Redl said, "I'm alive."

Another stunt nearly went wrong when he jumped over two cars in a tractor—which then snapped in half. However, Redl saw his stunts very calmly: "There is always a certain amount of risk," he said. "But if I was not confident about what I am doing I would not be doing it."

CORN PICKER TRACTOR

It might look like something from outer space, but this Massey-Harris machine is a corn picker. Corn, or maize, was picked largely by hand before World War II, though the Nichols and Shephard company did develop a mechanical picker in the 1920s. It was subsequently taken over by Oliver. After World War II, mechanical pickers attached to the front of tractors, with their distinctive "pincers" for safely gathering the plants without damaging the cobs, became the preferred method.

WHAT DOES THAT MEAN?

Articulated Steering

An articulated tractor is hinged in the middle— as is the case with an articulated truck, the idea here is to give extra maneuverability to a long vehicle. This has become the standard layout for high-power "supertractors," with articulated driveshafts in order to allow power delivery to both front and rear axles. Without articulation, tractors this big would be very unwieldy on the road and be unable to make tight headland turns.

Modern Classic Tractor

Harley-Davidson makes modern motorcycles that look like very old ones. If you have the money, you can buy a modern replica of an AC Cobra or Ford GT40 sports car. The same goes for tractors. In 1961, Tractors and Farm Equipment (TAFE) was set up in India, a joint venture between Massey-Ferguson and an Indian company. TAFE eventually broke away from MF but carried on making the old MF 35 under license. Over the years, TAFE updated and restyled the old tractor, but those who really want one can still buy the basic TAFE 35 DI in its old round-bonneted form, just like the original MF 35. It's even painted the same shade of red. Interestingly, the Indians see the 1950s-style 35 as outdated, but nostalgic farmers in Europe love it.

From India via the UK—the TAFE.

START 'EM YOUNG

It's a tradition on farms all over the world for the farmer's children to help out by driving the tractor. On private land, the property owner often has the right to grant driving privileges to youngsters. But even on the road, in some countries the minimum age for driving a tractor is less than that for driving a car. In the United Kingdom, provided the tractor is less than 8 feet (2.45 m) wide (and its trailer is no wider), a young tractor driver can take his or her driving test and gain a license at age sixteen, a year earlier than is permitted for driving a car.

Tractor drivers don't get old...

Combine Cross Regulations

Combine harvesters race on dirt tracks, too. Here are the classes, rules, and regulations:

★ **Standard Class** – Standard engine and belt drive are permitted, although nonstandard pulleys can be used.

★ **Special Class** – This class permits more powerful engines and beefier axles; no suspension is allowed.

★ **Free Class** – Full suspension and any other modification are allowed.

★ **All classes:** Speeds are limited to 50 mph (80 kph), all headers and unloading augers must be stripped off, and a roll bar and a racing harness for the driver must be added. All racing combines must have working brakes!

Specifications

Specifications of a typical modern tractor (2009 John Deere 8130)

» Outputs
Rated power (97/68EC)	225 hp
Max power (97/68EC)	245 hp
Max torque	742 pound-feet (1006 Nm) at 1600 rpm
Torque reserve	40 percent

» Engine
Type	Water-cooled in-line 6-cylinder diesel, 4 valves/cyl
Bore x stroke	4.66 x 5.35 inches (118.4 x 136 mm)
Capacity	549 cubic inches (9 L)
Aspiration	Variable geometry turbocharger, intercooled and aftercooled
Fueling	Electronic injection, common rail
Fuel capacity	180 gallons (681 L)

» Transmission options
AutoPowr	CVT with electronic engine/transmission management
Speed range	164 feet (50 m)/hour to 26 mph (42 kph)
Modes	4 modes: Manual, PTO, Heavy Draft Load Control, and Light Draft/Transport
Automatic power shift	16 forward, 5 reverse, full power shift and Field Cruise control

Speed range	8 field working speeds. 1–26 mph (2–42 kph) forward
Auto shifting	Shifts in relation to throttle position and load for transport and field applications

» PTO
Type	1,000 rpm, 20 spline or two-speed 1000/540 rpm
Engine speed at PTO speeds	2,000 rpm at 1,000, 1,820 rpm at 540

» Hydraulic system
Max pressure	200 bar
Max flow	44 gallons (167 L)/minute; optional 60 gallons (227 L)/minute
Electro-hydraulic control valves	Neutral, raise, lower, and float. Adjustable flow with temperature compensation. Load check valves and release assistors

» 3-Point Hitch
Category	Category 3N/3, optional Category 4N/4
Type	Electro-hydraulic with full electronic lower link draft sensing
Max lift at hooks	23,783 pounds (10,788 kg)
OECD lift capacity at 24 inches (610 mm)	20,985 pounds (9,519 kg)

» Steering and Brakes

Steering system	Hydrostatic power steering with ground drive backup system
Control	Tiltable, telescopic steering column with memory
Braking system	Power brakes with oil-cooled disc, hydraulically actuated and self-equalizing

» Front suspension (optional)

Type	Hydro-pneumatic, permanently active, automatic leveling, auto load compensation
Range/features	+/- 4.9 inches (125 mm) at each wheel, two double-acting hydraulic cylinders with damping
Front axle	Mechanical front-wheel drive with limited-slip differential

» Cab

Type	CommandView cab with ComfortCommand seat or active seat
Noise reduction	Passive noise reduction system, 72 decibels (A) in cab
Air system	Air conditioning or optional ClimaTrac
Display	CommandCenter display, corner post display, dashboard mini-pod, Hydraulic TouchSet panel

» Service Intervals/Quantities

Engine oil	375 hours/6.4 gallons (24.5 L)
Engine coolant	1,500 hours/10 gallons (40 L)
Transmission, final drive, and hydraulic oil	1,500 hours/42 gallons (160 L)

» Dimensions

L x W x H	18.3 x 8.13 x 10.8 feet (5.59 x 2.48 x 3.31 m)
With tire size	540/65 R30 and 650/65 R42
Minimum shipping weight	25,948 pounds (11,770 kg)

John Deere 8000 series is a typical modern tractor.

AD BREAK

Technical advertising appealed to a farmer's common sense. Often accompanied by cutaways revealing the tractor's inner workings, these ads would lay out, point by point, why this tractor was more powerful, more reliable, stronger, and more dependable than any other.

The hills are alive with the sound of tractors.

AIR VS. WATER COOLING

Air-cooled engines are rare on modern tractors (apart from the compacts) but in the past they have been used extensively. Deutz used air-cooled engines right into the modern era, and only went completely water-cooled with the all-new Agrotron in the 1990s. SAME of Italy also used air-cooled motors.

What are the pros and cons of air cooling and water cooling?

AIR COOLING
Pros: Simpler, lighter, cheaper to make, won't freeze up or boil over
Cons: Noisier, cooling fins can clog with dust, less-steady temperature control

WATER-COOLING
Pros: Quieter, easier to meet emissions limits, better temperature control, modern coolants won't freeze up
Cons: Heavier, more expensive, higher maintenance

Hey, cool it baby!

NO BRAKES

Brakes were a rare luxury on early tractors, for two reasons. The first was that manufacturers were more concerned with improving reliability; the second was that speeds were so low (usually below walking pace) that brakes weren't a big issue. Even the Fordson Model F had no brakes when it first appeared.

Of course, as speeds rose, brakes soon became standard (usually a transmission brake that operated on the rear wheels only). Four-wheel brakes only appeared after the 1980s, notably on SAME, Landini, and JCB machines.

Look out, no brakes!

EARLY FRONT DRIVER

Two-wheel drive means rear-wheel drive, right? Not for this Hackney Auto-Plow, hailing from 1911. The two big front wheels did the driving, and the single rear looked after the steering. Plows and other tillage tools were mid-mounted, not trailed, and the Hackney was even equipped with a power lift, operable from the driver's seat.

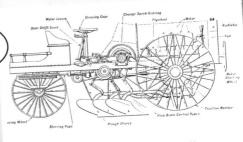

1911 Hackney "Auto-Plow"

Typical Maintenance Schedule

Tractor service intervals are measured in hours worked, not miles covered.

10-HOUR SERVICE:
- ✩ Check engine oil level.
- ✩ Check and if necessary clean the air cleaner pre-cleaner bowl. In very dusty conditions, check air filter element as well.
- ✩ On tractors with oil bath air cleaner, check level of sediment and change oil if it is dirty.
- ✩ Check screen washer level and top off if necessary.
- ✩ Check that all lights are working.

50-HOUR SERVICE:
- ✩ Complete 10-hour service jobs.
- ✩ In hot weather, check radiator coolant level and top off if necessary.
- ✩ Service the air cleaner.
- ✩ Lubricate grease points.
- ✩ Check tightness of wheel nuts.
- ✩ Check radiator fins and clean if necessary.

250- TO 300-HOUR SERVICE:
- ✩ Complete 10- and 50-hour service jobs
- ✩ Change engine oil and filter (at 500 hours on some tractors).
- ✩ Check brake and clutch pedal adjustment (tractors with mechanical linkage).
- ✩ Check oil levels in front axle, four-wheel drive, and transmission system.
- ✩ Clean battery terminals.
- ✩ Drain fuel filter sediment bowl of any water.

A tractor mechanic's work is never done.

500-HOUR SERVICE:
- ✩ Complete above-listed service jobs.
- ✩ Change diesel fuel filter.
- ✩ Change transmission oil filter (if present).

750- TO 1000-HOUR SERVICE:
- ✩ Change air filter element.
- ✩ Drain and flush engine cooling system.
- ✩ Change oil in transmission, front axle, and four-wheel-drive gearboxes.
- ✩ Change cab air filter element.

TOP TIPS
When using a tractor to consolidate a silage clamp, stay clear of the edges. Filled clamps should have sight rails.

Open wide...and a CVT makes it all so easy.

FENDT

CVT

WHAT DOES THAT MEAN?

CVT stands for "continuously variable transmission," and that's what this is: a transmission that offers an infinitely variable ratio set within certain limits. Almost universal on scooters and available on some cars, the CVT is fully automatic and makes the driving job much easier—there's no clutch to think about, or any need to select a ratio. Many high-horsepower tractors now come with CVT, and Fendt of Germany was one of the pioneer companies offering CVT, with its Vario. The company now has a complete lineup of Vario-equipped tractors, from the compact 200 to the 360 hp 936, the most powerful CVT tractor in the world.

MILESTONE TRACTORS

THE IVEL

NAME: IVEL

DATES: 1902–1913

WHY IS IT IMPORTANT? IT'S THE WORLD'S FIRST SMALL, LIGHTWEIGHT TRACTOR.

ENGINE TYPE: WATER-COOLED, TWIN-CYLINDER

POWER: 24 HP (INITIALLY 8 HP)

WEIGHT: 3,638 POUNDS (1650 KG)

PRICE: APPROXIMATELY $493/£300 (APPROXIMATELY $10,741/£6,528 TODAY)

GOOD POINTS: ITS LIGHT WEIGHT MADE IT EASIER TO MANAGE THAN ITS CONTEMPORARIES.

BAD POINTS: LACK OF DEVELOPMENT AFTER DAN ALBONE'S DEATH SAW IT FADE AWAY.

RANDOM FACT: THE IVEL WAS ALSO PROMOTED AS A FIRE ENGINE AND A MILITARY AMBULANCE.

HISTORY: Dan Albone, who lived in Buckinghamshire, England, at the turn of the twentieth century, was a racing cyclist, self-taught engineer, and prolific inventor. He made things, too, going into business as a cycle manufacturer (including tandems and the world's first ladies' frame) before turning his attention to tractors.

Like many of the tractor pioneers, Albone had grown up on a farm, and in 1901 he patented what he called the "agricultural motor." (He couldn't call it a tractor, because the term hadn't been invented yet.) Never one to waste time, he put the Ivel into production the following year.

What was new about the Ivel? Most other pioneer tractors were massive machines based on steam traction engine practice. The Ivel was a small three-wheeler weighing just 3,638 pounds (1,650 kg), manageable enough to be used on smaller farms. The horizontal-twin-cylinder engine was mid-mounted, with the cooling water tank at the rear, putting plenty of weight over the driving wheels.

But Dan Albone was not destined to be Britain's Henry Ford. At the time, few of the country's farms were ready for tractor power—the big estates still used steam engines and everyone else was wedded to horsepower. However, the Ivel was exported to eighteen countries, including Canada.

SMALL, PRAGMATIC, AND SLIGHTLY ECCENTRIC—
THAT WAS THE ENGLISH IVEL.

HENRY FORD

Most Important Tractor:
FORDSON MODEL F 1917–1928

Henry Ford came from farming stock. Although the young Henry had a fascination with engineering, he also kept an emotional attachment to the land (even if, later in life, this viewpoint had a distinctly rose-tinted quality).

From Car to Tractor

Given his background, it's hardly surprising that, once Ford's dream of creating a cheap mass-produced car (the Model T) became reality, he began thinking about a tractor. Within a few years, his company was the biggest car maker in the world, and he could afford to experiment. A number of companies were offering conversions to turn the T into a basic tractor. Ford thought he could do better, and he announced that he could produce a proper purpose-built tractor for the unheard-of price of $200/£122 (approximately $3,370/£2,048 today)—a true Model T for the fields. And, with the Fordson Model F, he did it.

Henry would later abandon the F in favor of more car production, but he retained a nostalgic affection for the rural way of life. It's ironic that he hankered for the fast-disappearing simpler life that his own successes had helped to destroy.

IRON HORSE

The Samson Iron Horse was aptly named. Controlled not by a steering wheel but by reins, it could be operated at a distance while the driver rode on a corn planter or binder.

Look more closely at the Iron Horse. It was a four-wheel-drive machine (in 1919!), with a chain final drive to each side. Each side could be controlled separately, so it was possible to run the tractor forward on one side and reverse on the other, allowing it to spin around.

GAUGES AND GADGETS

Every tractor driver has to be kept informed, so every tractor has at least one instrument to report what's going on under the hood. Few tractors have speedometers, but a far more useful informant is the tachometer, which indicates how fast the engine is spinning. The tachometer sometimes includes a speed reader as well.

Let me tell you everything.

You can't just tow me around—I've got a brain too!

Intelligent Implements

In the past, the technology used in plows, harrows, and so on trickled down from that used in tractor developments, but in the early twenty-first century implement-makers began coming up with innovations of their own.

New Systems on the Way

Walterscheid of Germany, for example, developed a new type of three-point linkage that replaced the lift rods and top link with hydraulic rams. That meant that the two fixed arms and lower links could work independently, while the hydraulic top link could automatically alter its length to adjust implement height for working or transport.

Implement-makers were also developing integrated control systems that allowed both implement and tractor to be controlled from the same unit. Amazone, Pottinger, and TeaJet all came up with systems that could "patch into" the Fendt Vario control unit. No doubt about it—the days of the dumb, towed implement were long gone.

TOP TIPS

Always disengage the PTO shaft and stop the engine before making any adjustment to a powered implement.

What? You call that a crop?

FORESTRY TRACTORS

Farm tractors have long been adapted for forestry work, for hauling trailers full of logs out of the forest. Because of the high haulage demands and difficult terrain, these have usually been four-wheel-drive conversions of standard tractors, or factory-fresh crawlers.

Ford conversion specialist County did good business selling its four-wheel-drive Fordson Major and, later, Super-6 for forestry work through the 1960s. The same was true of later County tractors through the 1970s. Some were fitted with a Brockhouse torque converter transmission.

Tractors With Sports Car Names

Ferrari – No connection with the more famous Ferrari. Specializes in small vineyard, turf, and farm tractors. The latest Cobram can be bidirectional (the driver can face either way).

Lamborghini – Ferruccio Lamborghini built tractors from 1947, long before he branched out into luxury sports cars. He first used army-surplus parts and later made his own air-cooled diesels. Now this manufacturer is part of the SAME-Deutz-Fahr group.

Porsche – Dr. Ferdinand Porsche and his son Ferry both designed tractors. The senior Porsche's was a basic single-cylinder Volkschlepper (a sort of farming equivalent to the Volkswagen) and the younger Porsche's was a twin-cylinder diesel launched in the late 1940s. Porsche soon sold its tractor interests to Allgeier, who built about twenty-five thousand Porsche tractors up to 1957.

Fancy a go in my Lamborghini?

REAR TRACK ADJUSTMENT METHODS

- Reversing the wheels
- Positioning rim clamps
- Rack and pinion adjustment
- Positioning the wheel hub
- Power adjustment

Road Roller

Not many tractors have been converted to road rollers—in fact, this is probably the only one. Ernest Doe & Sons, makers of the famous Doe Triple D tandem tractor, thought it would work, and built a prototype based on a Fordson Super Major. As well as the heavy rollers at each end, it had a fluid drive shuttle box for instant changes of direction (essential for a roller), plus a double-acting hydraulic ram to make those big front rollers steer.

The Doe roller never went into production—there was too much competition from existing rollers—and the prototype was leased to Cambridge University for building work. It was also used for that most English of jobs—rolling a cricket pitch.

Rollin', Rollin', Rollin...

TRACTOR SAFETY FIRST!

Get into the habit of following safe practices:
- ✪ Before getting into the tractor, check to make sure no one is nearby.
- ✪ Read the operator's manual.
- ✪ When stopping, apply the brakes evenly.
- ✪ When parking, lower all implements to rest on the ground.
- ✪ After parking, remove the ignition key.
- ✪ Do not tow start—use a booster battery.
- ✪ Never drive when tired or ill.
- ✪ Finally, use common sense!

WHY FORDSON, NOT FORD?

Henry Ford's Model F had to be made under the Fordson name, because, when production began in 1917, a "Ford" tractor already existed, made by a different company. Because Henry couldn't use his own name, Fordson (a shortened form of "Ford and Son") was the next best thing.

SHORT-TURN SHORTY

Was this the shortest tractor ever built? The Short Turn was built in the United States, between 1918 and 1920, and consisted of an almost-square platform supported by three wheels—two big driving wheels and a tiny front steerer, with a wheelbase of around 4 feet (1.2 m). The makers claimed 20/30 hp (20 hp at the drawbar, 30 hp at the belt), and the Short Turn sold for $1,500/£911 (approximately $18,701/£11,358 today).

No Mr Ford, you can't call it a Ford.

How a TRACTOR IS BUILT

CNH Global's factory in Basildon, England, is its biggest in Europe. The place covers 100 acres (40 hectares)—40 of them (16 hectares) roofed over—and builds 30,000 tractors of 100 or higher hp a year.

Engine and transmission are trucked in from other CNH plants in Europe, bolted together, and shipped across the factory by AGV (Auto Guided Vehicle).

Engine meets transmission—romantic, isn't it?

Robots don't get tired, but they're not that clever.

Painting is by robot in air-conditioned booths, but workers are there to spray the more intricate nooks and crannies. After painting, the whole thing gets oven-baked dry for two hours at 176°F (80°C).

Cab is put together as a subassembly, and, because most tractors are preordered, they are assembled to particular specs. Once complete, the cab is connected up to a clever machine that fools the cab into thinking its already mounted on a tractor. Every connection is tested in ten to twenty seconds.

Cab gets fooled by machinery.

Now it's starting to look like a tractor.

The Cab is lowered onto the painted drivetrain and fully connected up in three minutes. The complete tractor is designed to be easily assembled.

Oils and hydraulic fluid are added, air conditioning charged and wheels/tires added. The completed tractor gets a full predelivery inspection and rolling road test.

Let's see those wheels moving.

Ready for a life of hard toil.

Tractors are lined up outside the factory, waiting to be shipped out to a dealer. Over six thousand parts make up one tractor, now fully tested and ready to work.

Not Always New Holland

CNH's factory was actually built by Ford. Ford GB once made tractors at its big Dagenham car plant, but it found it was running out of space. In the early 1960s, with the new 6X worldwide tractors on the way, the company decided to build a brand-new factory on a Greenfield site. Work started in early 1962 and the first tractor left the gleaming new factory in May 1964. The factory has been making Ford and New Holland tractors ever since.

Do you remember the 60s?

An impressive six-pack!

Six-Wheel Tractors

Can a six-wheel tractor work? Valmet tried the idea in the early 1970s, the tractor's big rear wheels replaced by a bogie of four small ones. It had good traction, but it was too heavy (by about 2 tons, or 1.8 tonnes) to be an effective farm tractor, although a few were sold to the peat industry and for other industrial use.

A quarter of a century later, Fendt displayed this six-wheeler, a 540 hp six-wheel-drive machine with a road speed of 40 mph (65 kph), optional antilock brakes, and full suspension. It was also fully automatic, using two of Fendt's Vario transmission units. The Fendt six was a working prototype, not just a mockup, and the company claimed it had better traction and stability than a four-wheeler, on both road and field.

LINKAGE CARE TIPS

❖ Grease lift linkage and leveling box weekly.

❖ Check transmission oil level (or separate hydraulic reservoir, if there is one) weekly.

❖ Do not lubricate balls in lower links. This collects grit and causes rapid wear.

❖ Never turn a sharp corner with an implement still in the soil. This puts strain on the linkage.

❖ Never tow from the top link. This will cause the tractor to rear up and flip over backward. At 2 mph (3.2 kph), a tractor can rear 90 degrees in one second.

NOTHING NEW

The twenty-first-century JCB Fastrac Quadtronic has four-wheel drive and four-wheel steering, but there's nothing new about that. The Nelson tractor offered just the same facility (though maybe not quite so effectively) back in 1912. Powered by a four-cylinder 20/28 hp Wisconsin engine, it drove via a two-speed transmission to a double driving sheave, which in turn drove both front and rear axles via hardened chains.

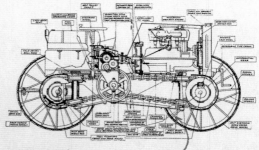

Four-wheel steering? Pah, had that in grandad's day.

Horsepower

Horsepower is a measure of the rate of work done, although torque (turning effort) is really a better measure of a tractor's pulling power. There are various measures of horsepower:

GROSS HORSEPOWER: Measured at the flywheel of a bare engine not yet installed in a tractor and with no power-sapping ancillaries (such as electrics, power-steering pump, or other devices).

NET HORSEPOWER: Measured at the flywheel of an engine equipped with all ancillaries.

PTO (POWER TAKEOFF) HORSEPOWER: Power at the tractor's power takeoff.

DRAWBAR HORSEPOWER: Power available at the drawbar for pulling implements.

PEAK BRAKE HORSEPOWER: Highest power developed without any engine speed limitation.

RATED HORSEPOWER: Power at the tractor's rated engine speed.

CONTINUOUS BRAKE HORSEPOWER: Rating recommended under continuous work.

WHAT DOES THAT MEAN?

Forget the fancy words, it's what horsepower does that counts.

Harvesting With Combine

The first combine harvesters were horse-drawn and then tractor-drawn, driven by the power takeoff. Then someone had the idea of equipping the combine with its own gasoline or diesel engine to power the grain separation. From there, it was a short step to make the combine self-propelled.

Tractors and Combines: A Powerful Partnership
This new invention didn't make the tractor redundant at harvest time. Combines do three jobs: cut the corn, separate the grain, and eject the straw. That's an impressive list of jobs for one pass, but what a combine can't do is store a whole day's harvest in its tank. To do so would make it far too heavy and unwieldy.

So tractors and trailers run a shuttle service, traveling alongside the combine to catch the grain. When the trailer is full, the tractor hauls it off to the silo (which could be some miles away) while the combine carries on working, storing grain in its tank until the next trailer comes along. The tractor and combine driver need to work together, traveling at exactly the same speed and ensuring that the trailer fills evenly.

TWO-PEDAL BRAKING
Tractors have two brake pedals—one for the left-hand brake, one for the front—to assist in tight turns. The pedals must be locked together when one is driving on the road, in order to ensure even braking.

Hey Charlie, mind you lock those brake pedals together.

Sisters are doing it for themselves.

Women On The Land

During both world wars, with the male farm workers being called up to fight, the British government recruited women to take their place. The Womens' Land Army was the result, often taking city girls with no experience in the countryside, giving them a month's training, and setting them to work on farms.

Many of the land girls learned to drive a tractor as part of the deal, usually a Fordson, plowing, harrowing, hauling, or doing any other job that was called for. The work was hard, but it was a life-changing experience for many. The American women in this picture may or may not be land girls, but they look happy enough.

TRACTORS ON US FARMS 1920–1950

YEAR	TRACTOR NUMBERS
1920	246,083
1925	505,933
1930	920,021
1940	1,567,430
1945	2,421,747
1950	3,609,281

Source: 1950 US Census of Agriculture

THE PEANUT DIESEL

There's nothing new about biofuels. Rudolph Diesel's very first diesel engine of 1895 ran on peanut oil.

JOHN DEERE MODEL D

DATES: 1923–1953

WHY IS IT IMPORTANT? CONFIRMED THE "JOHNNY POPPER" TWIN-CYLINDER AS JOHN DEERE'S ENGINE LAYOUT OF CHOICE.

ENGINE TYPE: WATER-COOLED, TWIN-CYLINDER, 508 CI (7.9 L)

POWER: 34.5/40 HP

WEIGHT: 8,125 POUNDS (3,693 KG)

PRICE: $1,000/£697 IN 1924 (APPROXIMATELY $12,613/£7,659 TODAY).

GOOD POINTS: SOLID AND RELIABLE, THE BACKBONE OF JOHN DEERE'S RANGE FOR THIRTY YEARS.

BAD POINTS: LATER OVERTAKEN BY LIGHTER, MORE ADAPTABLE TRACTORS.

RANDOM FACT: FIRST SUCCESSFUL TRACTOR TO CARRY THE JOHN DEERE NAME.

HISTORY: John Deere owes its position in the market to this tractor. Well, almost. The company came to tractors late, trying various formats before buying up the Waterloo Gasoline Engine Company and its Waterloo Boy tractor. But, by the early 1920s, the Waterloo was sadly outdated.

Rather than start from scratch, John Deere built on the Boy's good points. The Model D had a low-revving twin-cylinder engine and two-speed transmission, but with an all-new chassis, and the transmission was fully enclosed.

Now, on the face of it, this was already looking a little tired compared to rival tractors with four-cylinder motors and multispeed transmission. But the farmers loved the new John Deere. Why? Because that easygoing twin-cylinder engine would haul a heavy plow through sticky soil without faltering. Sure, it only had two forward speeds, but it didn't really need any more than that. The John Deere was reliable, too, and earned its nickname—"Johnny Popper"; for many farmers it became like one of the family.

Tens of thousands were made, and the Model D stayed in production right through to 1953. Other Deeres came and went, but the faithful D was always there.

MODEL D WAS JOHN DEERE'S FAVORITE GREAT-UNCLE,
THE COMPANY'S BACKBONE FOR THIRTY YEARS.

Do your plowing in complete luxury!

LUXURY CAB

Specification for the Case Magnum Luxury cab:

+ OPTIMA SEAT
+ ADJUSTABLE FOR RIDE FIRMNESS, LUMBAR SUPPORT, AND BACKREST ANGLE
+ SWIVELS TO LEFT OR RIGHT
+ ARMREST CONTROLS SWIVEL WITH SEAT
+ HEATED
+ AUTOMATIC TEMPERATURE CONTROL
+ TILTABLE STEERING WHEEL
+ POWER OUTLETS (SIX)
+ DOME LIGHTS
+ POSITIVE RESPONSE SUSPENSION (reacts five hundred times per second to give smooth ride)
+ RED LEATHER SEATS
+ LEATHER INSTRUCTIONAL SEAT
+ LEATHER-WRAPPED STEERING WHEEL AND THROTTLE LEVER
+ LEATHER RIGHT-HAND ARMREST
+ CARPETED FLOOR MAT

Stamps

Postage stamps come in all shapes, sizes, colors, and subjects. Of course, you might expect a range of monarchs, sportsmen, and national icons, but tractors have made an appearance on the postage stamp, too. The subjects depicted on stamps are a good measure of what has meaning to the population of the country that issued them. Hence this stamp from Pakistan—in this mainly agricultural country, tractors are a part of everyday life for most of the population.

Tractors by post.

THE STEAM FAIR IN NUMBERS

Dorset Steam Fair is Europe's largest gathering of steam power, and old vehicles in general—including tractors, both static and working.

- ✪ 120 catering units
- ✪ 200 working steam engines
- ✪ 1,000 trade stands
- ✪ 2,000 exhibits
- ✪ 9,000 tents/caravans overnight
- ✪ 200,000 day visitors
- ✪ 800,000 Website hits (Jan–May 2008)
- ✪ Biggest-ever exhibit = 100 ton (90 tonne) steam locomotive

THE MOST WHEAT HARVESTED
608 tons (551.6 tonnes) in eight
hours, by New Holland CR9090
with 10.7 m Varifeed Head,
on September 26, 2008, in
Northumberland, England.
It covered 132.2 acres (53.5
hectares) and used 3.5 gallons
(13.3 L) of diesel per 2.47 acres
(1 hectare).

Snow Tractors

They're not farm tractors in the conventional sense, but fully tracked snow machines such as the Tucker Sno Cat and the Pisten Bulley have also been used well away from the snow line. Their wide tracks, made of steel, aluminum, or rubber, spread the weight of the tractor and help prevent it from getting bogged down. So they have also been used on marshy ground and over soft peat bogs, on tidal mudflats such as the Wadden Sea off the coast of Holland and Germany. Snow tractors have even been put to work leveling piles of sugar beet.

Gimme more, gimme more!

SEVEN-YEAR ITCH?

Tractor sales in the US followed a pattern in which they peaked every six to seven years from the late 1950s: 1959, 1966, 1973 and 1979 were all good years. This cycle was rudely interrupted by the recession of 1980s and early 1990s.

There's snow business like tractor business!

May not look radical, but it was.

World's First Tractor

The world's first working tractor using a gasoline engine was built in 1892 by one John Froelich from Iowa. A Van Duzen engine was mounted on a wooden chassis with traction engine running gear. Froelich hitched it up to a Case thresher and worked it for 52.5 days, threshing sixty-two thousand bushels of wheat, with no major breakdowns. The tractor was born.

Grandfather of the Green Machine

As any John Deere fan will tell you, Froelich's tractor was the grandfather of the green and yellow machines. John Froelich set up the Waterloo company in 1893, which was bought by Deere in 1918 and got them started in the tractor business.

Which Suspension?

As tractor suspension systems multiplied in the late 1990s, the big question was: Which was best? Front suspension only (offered by Case and John Deere as an option), all-around suspension as standard (JCB Fastrac), or cab suspension (pioneered by Renault)?

Tests by Profi tractor magazine found that driver impressions varied widely, but it did come to the following conclusions:

★ **Cab suspension only:** Better comfort; little effect on handling

★ **Front-axle suspension with cab suspension:** Better handling; better comfort

★ **Full suspension:** The optimum system, with the best handling and cab comfort

★ **Mounted plow and weighted front end:** Reduced shocks in the cab by 30 percent

Springs are so last year, don't you think?

THE SOVIETS LOVED FORDSONS

The Soviet Union became a prolific builder of tractors, but in its early years was dependent on American imports. Of the country's tractors, twenty-seven thousand were imported in 1924 to 1927, and by then more than 98 percent of tractors working in the USSR were American.

WHO WAS SNOOPY?

"Snoopy," "Anteater," "Worm," or even "Land Shark"—the International 2+2 55 series was called by all of these nicknames, thanks to its extra-long snout. It was unveiled in 1979, a new take on the theme of a pivot-steer supertractor. The cab was mounted behind the pivot-steer, not in front, and the engine was mounted well over the front axle for better weight distribution. This was also the only pivot-steer tractor with adjustable-width axles. The result, claimed International Harvester, was the maneuverability of a two-wheel-drive tractor with the traction of four-wheel drive. And few could argue with a turning radius of just 16 feet (4.8 m), something that many conventional tractors could not match. The traction claims proved well-founded, too, thanks to those big, equal-sized wheels (though it was found that the tight turning radius meant there wasn't room to fit duals on the front).

The Snoopys proved a hit with American farmers in their first two years, but eventually they were dragged down by International Harvester's problems as a company.

What's up, Charlie Brown?

WHAT DOES THAT MEAN?

Electronic Linkage Control

Electronic controls of the three-point hitch are now standard on most modern tractors, replacing the traditional levers, springs and rams. A lot of farmers were skeptical when ELC first appeared in the 1980s, thinking that this was just one more thing that could go wrong, but electronic control has proved reliable in practice. And there are plenty of advantages. ELC provides much more precise automatic control of the linkage—sensors report the exact position of the lower link arms and external lift rams while electronically operated control valves allow for swift adjustments. ELC also means linkage controls can be placed where they are most convenient in the cab and reduce noise levels.

Most Powerful Tractors Ever

In the early 1970s, there seemed to be no end to the tractor power race. Bigger was always better, according to accepted wisdom, and if a 500 hp tractor could work faster and more efficiently than a 400 hp, then a 600 hp would surely be better still.

Versatile of Canada had made its name with big supertractors like these, and in 1976 the company built a machine that topped them all. It was Big Roy, an eight-wheeler, powered by a Cummins inter-cooled six-cylinder diesel that delivered 600 hp at 2100 rpm.

Even Versatile's tough transmission couldn't cope with this much power, so a new six-speed unit was designed. At 30 feet (9.1 m) long and 11 feet (3.3 m) high, and tipping the scales at just over 25 tons (22.6 tonnes), Big Roy was a monster for the prairies. All of its eight wheels were driven, and the fuel tank held 463 gallons

(1,752 L) of diesel. But only one Big Roy was ever made—the 1970s recession saw to that.

A 1,000 hp Tractor

Meanwhile, Ron Harmon at Big Bud was dreaming of building the world's first 1,000 hp tractor, and in 1978 he did just that. The 16V-747 was based on the same concept as any big pivot-steer tractor, but it was powered by a 1464 cubic inch (24 L) V16 Detroit Diesel—rated at 760 hp, it could be turned up to the magic four-figure number. Special tires and a new transmission had to be designed to cope with it all.

Like the Big Roy, only one 747 (an apt name) was made, although it proved capable of prodigious work rates—its owner claimed it had paid for itself in just two years.

There's no substitute for cubes (or horsepower).

Tractors Don't Just Work On Farms

Life's a beach.

✪ HEAVY HAULAGE
Making use of the modern tractor's tremendous hauling power and higher road speeds. Some of these road tugs spend their entire working lives on blacktop.

✪ BOAT RECOVERY
Hauling boats from shallow water and up the beach. Often seen in Europe, with old, battered tractors doing the job.

Fancy a paddle?

Much better than a gnome!

✪ FISH STALL
It's true. In Holland, one tractor is used to take a portable fish stall along the beach.

✪ A BUS
In northern Germany, a big New Holland hauls a trailer load of people out to a nearby island at low tide.

✪ GARDEN FEATURE
Can you think of a better lawn decoration than this one, spotted in Connecticut?

✪ HARVESTING BAIT
Another beach tractor, this one harvesting bait for fishing. The seagulls seem to have caught on.

Also:
- ❖ Joy rides around the farm on open days
- ❖ A winter project to keep a man busy and out of his wife's hair
- ❖ A way of meeting people
- ❖ Free entry to steam fairs (as an exhibitor)

I think it's stalled!

PART OF THE FAMILY

Farms often stay in the family for generations, and the same is true of tractors.

Roger Bartlett has driven this tractor, man and boy.

Tractor: 1959 International B450
Family: The Bartletts of Dorset
Hours: 23,000
History: The B450 worked a 200-acre (80 hectare) dairy farm when new, but spent most of its life as part of Roger Bartlett's thriving contracting business—ditching, cultivating, plowing, and making water deliveries. In fifty years, it used three sets of pistons and liners, needed the gear selector shafts repaired, but had no other major replacements.

"A tractor is like an animal—look after it, and it'll repay you."

Tractor: 1939 Allis-Chalmers Model A
Family: The Barlows of Cheshire
Hours: Over 30,000
History: This tractor worked as a threshing contractor for much of its life, and was occasionally used for pulling out tree stumps! Over seventy years, it proved very reliable, still with the original piston rings, valves, and clutch. It's obviously been well looked after by four generations of Barlows. It was retired in 1966 (when combines made thresher-tractors obsolete) and given a light restoration in the mid-1970s. Concours Trophy winner.

Like father, like son.

"Oh, we'll never sell it—it'll stay in the family for sure."

"I'd like to pass it on to my kids—keep it in the family."

This Case is on its third generation Davis.

Tractor: 1944 Case SC
Family: The Davises of Shropshire
Hours: Not known
History: This Case has been used for plowing, baling, and mowing, plus threshing and towing a Ransome trailed combine. Retired in 1968 after clutch failure, then restarted by Steve Davis (third generation), who still uses it for some sawing and the occasional plowing match. The engine has never been apart.

In the 1920s and 1930s crawlers were the thing to have.

CRAWLERS

Four-wheel drive means that few modern tractors have crawler tracks, but in the 1920s and 1930s some farmers did pay extra for a crawler. In very wet soil, a crawler had far more pulling capacity than an equivalent steel- or rubber-wheeled tractor. They also spread the weight of the tractor over a larger area, reducing the risk of ruts and compacted soil. And on steep land, the extra grip improved stability and safety. To meet farmers' needs, Caterpillar even produced two small tracked tractors, the Ten and Fifteen, specifically for farmers.

The US was the biggest market for crawlers of all types in the 1920s and 1930s. Although Caterpillar was the market leader, it faced competition from Cletrac and Monarch, not to mention crawlers from such wheeled tractor makers as Allis-Chalmers, John Deere, and International Harvester.

Why Were Allis-Chalmers Tractors Orange?

One story goes like this: Allis-Chalmers boss Harry Merritt was on a business trip in the 1920s when he spotted some wild poppies in a California field. He was so taken by their striking color that he picked a bunch, took it back to the factory, and decreed that from now on all Allis-Chalmers tractors be painted this shade.

The less-romantic version is that A-C produced a new tractor for United Tractors and Farm Equipment (a Chicago-based cooperative) whose color was orange, and A-C simply changed its own shade to suit. Take your pick.

Any color you like as long as it's orange.

Vineyard tractors earn their keep in wine country.

VINEYARD TRACTORS

Vineyard tractors have to be small in order to squeeze between the vines, be very maneuverable in order to make the tight turn at the end of each row, and have excellent traction, as vines are often grown on steep south-facing slopes.

Small modern tractors can be adapted to suit, with narrow-tracked versions offered by many of the major manufacturers. But the really specialist vineyard tractors hail from Italy. (Did you really expect them to be from Britain, Norway, or Sweden?) These are generally low-profile, narrow machines, with articulation for very tight turns and four-wheel drive for traction. Power comes from a two-, three-, or four-cylinder diesel.

The Steel Wheel Problem

Early tractors used steel wheels fitted with spade lugs to provide traction. This was all very well in the field, but, as paved roads began to spread across the United States, they proved damaging to the new road surfaces and gave a very slow, uncomfortable ride, at 5 mph (8 kph) if you were lucky. Some states actually banned steels on roads.

Solid rubber tires didn't damage the blacktop, but they gave very poor traction in the field. Removable lugs and bolt-on "road bands" (a smooth band that fitted over the lugs) were other solutions, but they were laborious to remove and replace. The same was true of chains on solid rubber. Not until Allis-Chalmers and Firestone launched the pneumatic tractor tire in 1932 could tractors finally travel on blacktop with reasonable speed and comfort.

Steel wheels were dropped because of the damage they did to the roads.

> "There are only three things that can kill a farmer: lightning, rolling over in a tractor, and old age."
> Bill Bryson

You can't learn to plow in a morning.

HOW TO PLOW

Look after your plow, and it'll look after you.

PLOW CARE TIPS

❖ Grease all lubrication points during the plowing season.

❖ Change all soil wearing parts when worn. This is especially important for the shares, because blunt shares make the plow harder to pull.

❖ Check to make sure that all nuts and bolts are tight.

❖ At the season's end, replace worn parts, spray bright surfaces with a corrosion inhibitor, and store the plow under cover.

Pre-Plowing Checks

Check to make sure that:

✓ the plow is properly attached
✓ the tractor wheels are on a suitable track setting for the furrow width
✓ pitch adjustment is correct
✓ moldboards are parallel to each other
✓ shares are in good condition
✓ discs and skimmers are deep enough to do their job
✓ the plow suits the tractor (in other words, that it can be pulled with the correct amount of wheel slip)

PLOWING TECHNIQUES

There are two basic alternatives: systematic plowing (backward and forward) or round and round (just what it sounds like).

❖ **For systematic plowing**, first plow a headland marking furrow all around the field, leaving a 16-foot (8 m) headland for a three-furrow plow. Divide the field into sections ("lands") with shallow markings for furrows and ridges. Start plowing by round and round the first ridge, and then between the two neighboring ridges—this reduces idle running time at the headland to a minimum.

❖ **For round-and-round plowing**, work literally around from the center of the field to the outside, or the other way around. To keep a level field, do it from the center out one year and from the outside to the center the next, and so on.

TOP TIPS

To keep to a straight line (assuming you have no GPS assistance), pick a reference point at the far side of the field and head for that.

Even with all the modern gizmos, plowing is still a skilled job.

FERGUSON MODEL A

DATES: 1936–1938

WHY IS IT IMPORTANT? IT WAS THE FIRST TRACTOR WITH THE FERGUSON THREE-POINT HITCH.

ENGINE TYPE: WATER-COOLED, FOUR-CYLINDER, 133 CI (2.1 L)

POWER: 20 HP

WEIGHT: 3,638 POUNDS (1,650 KG)

PRICE: APPROXIMATELY $401/£244 (APPROXIMATELY $6,006/£3,650 TODAY)

GOOD POINTS: SUPERB FIELD PERFORMANCE FOR ITS WEIGHT AND POWER.

BAD POINTS: IT WAS EXPENSIVE AND NEEDED ITS OWN IMPLEMENTS.

RANDOM FACT: A SINGLE SPANNER (11/16 AND 1 1/16 AF) WOULD FIT ALL NUTS AND BOLTS NEEDED FOR ADJUSTMENT ON THE FERGUSON AND ITS IMPLEMENTS.

HISTORY: Harry Ferguson perfected his revolutionary three-point hitch in the early 1930s. He also designed a tractor to go with it. It was a radical tractor for its time, a squat little thing with modest power, whose secret weapon was that famous hitch.

Onlookers scoffed that a little tractor with a mere 20 hp could do any serious work, but the three-point hitch gave the Ferguson superb traction, especially in tricky conditions and hilly terrain. In one competitive plowing demonstration, which was almost called off because it was snowing, the big, heavy tractors lost traction one by one and dropped out. Only two kept going and finished the job: the complicated Massey-Harris GP, and the Ferguson.

So was the Model A about to take over the world? Sadly, it was not to be. At $401/£224, it cost approximately $138/£84 more than a Fordson, and the farmer had to buy special Ferguson implements to go with it, because standard hauled tools wouldn't fit the three-point hitch. And, despite its performance in the field, many farmers were distrustful of something so radical.

The Model A sold well in hilly areas like Scotland and Norway, but it couldn't compete with the big boys. Still, its legacy as the first three-point-equipped tractor helped Harry Ferguson reach his handshake agreement with Henry Ford. And that's when the Ferguson System really hit the big time.

NOT A MODEL A, BUT A LATER FERGUSON TE. SAME LINEAGE,
SAME INSPIRATION, SAME THREE-POINT HITCH.

Determining Ballast

Two factors are key in determining how much ballast a tractor needs in order to achieve optimum wheel slip—horsepower and speed. Higher speeds generally mean less ballast, because a faster rolling tire has less time to deform each patch of soil. At lower speeds, more ballast is required, so how much ballast the tractor needs obviously depends on what job is being tackled.

How to Find the Right Ballast
At 5 mph (8 kph), the ideal total tractor weight, including ballast, is about 95 to 110 pounds (43 to 50 kg) per engine horsepower (though the manufacturer will list specific recommendations for each model in the handbook). That will produce the optimum wheel slip percentage. But look at the effect of speed: at 4 mph (6.4 kph), the ideal weight is around 160 pounds (72 kg) per horsepower, and at 6 mph (9.6 kph) little more than 100 pounds (45 kg) per horsepower.

Measuring Wheel Slip
To measure wheel slip, compare the number of wheel turns over a fixed distance, looking at the tractor unloaded and under full load. Or compare the distance the tractor travels for a fixed number of wheel turns—again, unloaded and under full load. Of course, if the tractor is ultramodern and packed with electronics, it will probably have a wheelspin indicator in the cab.

Want to do this right? You'll need ballast.

A Tractor Movie

There are many tractor movies—films of tractors working—shown at steam fairs all over the world and available on DVD. But *Earthworm Tractors* (1936) may be the only movie ever to have starred a tractor.

The star was a Caterpillar crawler, and Alexander Botts (played by Joe E. Brown) was the costar, a natural-born tractor salesman (or so he thinks) who actually knows nothing about tractors. His desperate efforts to sell a tractor to grumpy lumberman Mr. Johnson (who is clearly in the anti-tractor camp) result in mayhem, with Johnson's daughter providing the love interest. It ends well, but the tractor definitely upstages the actors.

I think Joan Plowright is in this one!

Tractor schizophrenia?
This one runs on gasoline
AND diesel.

International Harvester's Gasoline/Diesel Hybrid

In the twenty-first century, everyone's talking about gasoline-electric hybrid cars in a bid to cut emissions and fuel consumption, but this tractor is a very different sort of hybrid. The International Harvester WD-40 started up on gasoline but ran on diesel.

Early diesels were notoriously tricky to start from cold, and manufacturers tried all sorts of tricks to make the job easier. In the end, efficient glow plugs did the business. But back in 1936, these weren't the obvious answer, and International Harvester's solution was an engine equipped with two fueling systems in parallel: spark plugs and magneto on one

side; diesel pump and injectors on the other. To start this hybrid engine, one turned a lever to open a small valve in each combustion chamber, reducing the compression ratio enough for the start-up on gasoline. Once the engine had run for 45 seconds, these valves automatically closed, increasing compression and allowing the operator to open the diesel fuel lever. And then the WD-40 was ready for a diesel-fueled day's work, at which it was 50 percent more economical than the straight gas-powered WK-40. International Harvester reckoned it could plow 15 to 20 acres

(6 to 8 hectares) a day, on 15 to 20 gallons (56 to 75 L) of fuel: a superefficient hybrid of its day.

STEAM EFFICIENCY

Steam engine efficiency improved dramatically in the 1850s. See the RASE Fuel Efficiency Trial results below.

COAL BURNED PER
HORSEPOWER-HOUR

Year	Performance of winning engine
1849	11.50 POUNDS
1850	7.56 POUNDS
1852	4.66 POUNDS
1853	4.32 POUNDS
1854	4.55 POUNDS
1855	3.70 POUNDS

TRACTORS IN MINIATURE

Perfect Replicas

Pedal tractors have been around for decades, big enough for a child to sit in and pedal along. But these are different—they have real motors, and some of them can do real work. In the 1970s, Malcolm Willis, a farmer in Dorset, southern England, set about making a miniature tractor for his two sons. It was a half-scale Field Marshall Series III, perfect in every detail, and powered by a 100 cc Honda gasoline engine.

Others soon followed, and, when he was old enough, Malcolm's son Andy started building miniature tractors of his own. Others included more Field Marshalls, a crawler-tracked Fowler, and an electric-powered Fordson, all of them strict replicas of the real things, only smaller. Andy later built a half-scale Marshall MP-6, complete with 12 hp Yanmar diesel engine and four-speed transmission; the family use it for spiking the lawn.

Learner Tractors

The Willis's aren't the only people to have made small replica tractors, though Cec Crooks's machines were different. Powered by small car engines, and much bigger than half scale, each one was powerful enough to do real work. He made around one hundred of them, aping the full-size style of a Massey-Ferguson 35, Minneapolis-Moline, Allis-Chalmers WD-45, various Fordsons, Oliver 90, a White, a Field Marshall, and a Massey-Harris.

All were based on a standard chassis, and Cec made up the tinwork out of fiberglass and filler, working from photographs of the originals. He found the engines (Vauxhall Viva, Austin Metro, and similar units), gearboxes, wheels, and axles in scrapyards. Throttled down at a safe speed, they proved very popular with children, and the replica White could pull a one-furrow plow!

Small but perfectly formed.

Turf Tractors

Tractors aren't just used on farms. They've been used as runaround tugs in factories, for hauling heavy loads on the road, and for hauling boats up the beach. Big expanses of grass need tractors too—baseball and football pitches, in fact sports arenas of all kinds, golf courses, and country estate lawns.

Turf, or lawn, tractors come in many shapes and sizes, up to around 50 hp. They don't have the farm tractor's aggressively treaded tires; instead, they use grass tires with a smoother tread that won't damage the surface or dig into the soil. Turf tractors may be purpose-built compact machines, or adapted versions of small general-purpose tractors.

Turf wars—grass tires + low clearance = a turf tractor.

Bulldog—The Euro-Standard Tractor

* **Bubba** – Italy (1925–1926)
* **Deutz MTH 222** – Germany (1926)
* **Baumi** – Germany (1927)
* **Landini** – Italy (1926–1950s)
* **Orsi** – Italy (Late 1920s–1934)
* **Cassani** – Italy (1927)
* **MAIS** – Germany (1928)
* **Mercedes-Benz** – Germany (1928–early 1930s)
* **Marshall** – Britain (1929–1957)
* **McDonald** – Australia (1930–1950s)
* **Vierzon** – France (1932–late 1950s)
* **Le Percheron** – France (1940s–1957)
* **KL Bulldog** – Australia (1940s–1953)
* **Ursus** – Poland (late 1940s–late 1950s)

If there was ever a European standard design of tractor, then it was the Lanz Bulldog. The Bulldog was launched in 1921, using a horizontal single-cylinder semi-diesel engine. Also known as a "hot-bulb" engine, this was a very slow revving unit that was reliable, low maintenance, and able to run on just about any fuel.

It was also crude, unsophisticated, and inefficient, but the semi-diesel's reliability saw it being adopted by manufacturers all over Europe and even in Australia, most of them following the lines of the original Lanz Bulldog. Starting one of these tractors was an art in itself, as the cylinder head had to be heated with a blowlamp until it was hot enough for the engine to start.

By the mid-1950s, the single-cylinder semi-diesel had been overtaken by a new generation of small four-cylinder full diesels, and by the end of the decade most, if not all, of them were gone.

The distinctive bark of a diesel single gradually gave way to the blander rattle of a multicylinder.

The Lanz Bulldog was copied or built under license more than any other tractor. (The Marshall was influenced by Lanz, but not a semi-diesel.) Here's a list:

* **Werewolf** – Germany (1924–1926)
* **HSCS** – Hungary (1924–1950s)
* **MAVAG** – Hungary (dates not known)

Copy cat—French Vierzon was just one of many Bulldog lookalikes.

ADJUSTABLE TREADS: THE WHY AND HOW

When a farmer is cultivating crops planted in rows, like cotton or corn, it's obviously essential that the tractor wheels run between the rows, not over them. This was where the International Farmall scored in the late 1920s, with axles of adjustable width that could adapt to rows of different spacings.

Other manufacturers soon followed suit, although adjusting the axles wasn't a five-minute job—the rear wheels had to be moved in and out along splines. In 1955, Allis-Chalmers brought engine power to the job with Power Shift. The tractor's own power was used to move the rear wheels in or out along spiral rails.

Jack up, crank out, drive on.

Bidirectional Tractors

Bidirectional tractors can work equally well backward or forward, with the driver able to face in either direction. In fact, with bidirectionals, there is really no such thing as forward or backward!

Many tractor manufacturers offer 180-degree swiveling seats on conventional tractors, with the steering wheel and major controls either moving with the seat or duplicated. One of the few Irish-built tractors was a bidirectional—the Moffett MFT (Multi-Function Tractor), which was offered in the 1990s.

Perhaps the most spectacular bidirectional tractor is the Claas Xerion, whose cab is raised hydraulically at the touch of a button, swivels 180 degrees, and moves to the rear or center of the tractor as required.

It All Started with Versatile
Who made the first bidirectional tractor?

Versatile pioneered the breed back in 1977, with its 150. The entire cab swiveled 180 degrees so that the tractor could be used as a loader in one direction or a conventional tractor in the other direction. It was such a good idea that it became a permanent feature of Versatile's line, and it remained in production even after New Holland took over the company.

Is this thing going backward or forward?

Small And Streamlined

Orchards need a special sort of tractor—one that is narrow enough to fit between the rows of trees and won't damage the fruit.

American manufacturers led the way in the 1920s and 1930s by adapting farm tractors, reducing the overall height by removing vertical exhaust pipes and air cleaner stacks, and fitting smoother, more flowing bodywork that would gently brush aside the fruit-laden branches. After World War II, orchard tractors became more specialized, with a lower profile and with very narrow tracks to squeeze into modern orchards. The same is true of vineyard machines, and many manufacturers offer specific vineyard or orchard tractors.

Mind those grapes!

Specific Fuel Consumption

WHAT DOES THAT MEAN?

Car or truck fuel consumption is quoted in miles per gallon (mpg) or liters per 100 km (l/100 km), which is a simple measure of the distance traveled by road per unit of fuel. But that won't do for a tractor, whose fuel consumption will vary wildly according to the job it's doing, and whether it's on the road or in the field. Much more relevant is the amount of fuel consumed for a given amount of work. So the unit of fuel is divided by the power delivered (whether through the PTO at rated speed or in a particular gear when hauling at rated speed). With fuel measured by weight, this gives a more relevant figure for tractor efficiency—the metric unit is grams of fuel per kilowatt hour (g/kWh).

TRACTOR AS VILLAIN

In American folklore, tractors are often portrayed fondly, either as pioneers of Midwest farming or as part of the family. But in John Steinbeck's masterpiece novel *The Grapes of Wrath*, the story opens with a tractor demolishing the family farmstead. This is a flip side of the tractor's image: a tool of the ruthless modern world, destroying livelihoods and homes.

Those grapes are going feel my wrath!

TRACTORS TAKE OVER

Number of tractors produced and horses or mules on US farms,
1931-1950

YEAR	TRACTORS WHEELED	CRAWLERS	GARDEN TRACTORS	TOTAL	HORSES/MULES (MILLS
1931	61,940	7,089	2,675	71,704	18.5
1935	138,084	18,774	4,273	161,131	16.7
1940	249,434	24,762	9,350	283,546	14.5
1945	244,430	44,872	27,966	317,268	12.0
1946	258,274	25,902	118,237	402,413	11.1
1947	433,334	37,295	172,938	643,567	10.1
1948	529,587	39,412	184,624	753,623	9.3
1949	555,523	44,613	126,839	726,975	8.5
1950	498,768	43,680	151,198	693,646	7.8

FIT FOR PURPOSE?

Nearly all farm tractors are designed to cope with plowing fields, which makes sense. Or does it? In practice, plowing only lasts for a few weeks each year, and the rest of the time the tractor does much lighter, less demanding jobs. So any farm with more than one tractor should really invest in a lightweight machine that will do road haulage or light field work more economically than a "plow-first" tractor.

AD BREAK

At first glance, it looks as though the advertiser of this Hart-Parr was trying to suggest that any customer would be watched over by the Almighty. But no, it's Old Father Time, looking on approvingly as the tractor saves its owner precious hours.

MILESTONE TRACTORS

MINNEAPOLIS-MOLINE COMFORTRACTOR

DATES: 1938–1940

WHY IS IT IMPORTANT? IT WAS THE FIRST TRACTOR WITH A GLAZED CAB AND LUXURY FITTINGS.

ENGINE TYPE: WATER-COOLED, FOUR-CYLINDER, 283 CI (4.6 L)

POWER: 38 HP

WEIGHT: 6,000 POUNDS (2,722 KG)

PRICE: $2,155/£1,311 (APPROXIMATELY $32,965/£20,048 TODAY)

GOOD POINTS: COMFY, WEATHERPROOF CAB; 40 MPH (64 KPH) ROAD SPEED.

BAD POINTS: TOO EXPENSIVE FOR 1930S FARMERS.

RANDOM FACT: EQUIPMENT INCLUDED A CIGAR LIGHTER.

HISTORY: A heater, comfortable seat, and weatherproof cab—today we take all these things for granted on a modern tractor, but it was radical stuff back in 1938, when Minneapolis-Moline launched the "Comfortractor." Market research told them that more than 50 percent of farmers would like a factory-outfitted cab.

Minneapolis-Moline's response was indeed radical. The Comfortractor UDLX was sleek and streamlined, better looking than some cars of the day, and very well appointed. As well as the heater, there were windshield wipers (and defroster), a radio, two seats, full instrumentation with an electric clock, a roof light, and a cigar lighter.

Under the skin, it shared much with MM's more basic tractors, but the four-cylinder motor had an electric starter and was retuned to accept leaded gasoline. Best of all, a special five-speed transmission allowed shifting on the go and was geared for the dizzy road speed of 40 mph (64 kph)! Yet, the UDLX could still plow a field like any other tractor. In theory, one could do a day's work out in the field, hose the tractor down, and then drive it into town for the evening.

At $2,155 (£1,311), the Comfortractor was twice the price of an equivalent cab-less John Deere or International Harvester, and just 150 were sold. Still, it has to be one of the most stylish tractors ever built.

CAR, TRUCK, OR TRACTOR? YOU DECIDE.

Unimog was the most successful tractor-truck.

TRACTOR TRUCKS

Tractors that can carry and haul big loads, plow a field, and be used as general road transport have been around for a long time. The ideal is the ultimate all-around farm vehicle, which might do some field work in the morning, head out to the feed merchant after lunch to pick up a ton of supplies, do some road hauling in the late afternoon, and maybe even be driven to the movies in the evening. Tractor-trucks have always been a compromise, and, given the range of more specialized tractors available, this ultimate all-around vehicle looks unlikely to make a big comeback.

EARLY TRACTOR TRUCKS

In the United Kingdom, Saunderson produced a three-wheeled transport tractor back in 1906. According to the maker, it could carry 2 tons (1.8 tonnes) on the load bed, and haul another 2 tons on a trailer behind. The bed could be manually tipped, and Saunderson reckoned that its Universal tractor was a great all-purpose replacement for a team of two or three horses.

Three years later, Avery, in the United States, was offering its own farm truck. With 12 to 36 hp at 1,000 to 1,500 rpm, it came equipped with a belt pulley and drawbar. It was able to pull three 14-inch (35 cm) plows or carry 3 tons (2.7 tonnes) on the load bed (though maybe not at the same time). Still, when the farm truck was used for plowing, ballast had to be placed over drive wheels, since the Avery was two-wheel drive. For driving on hard roads, wooden plugs could be fitted to the wheels; for really soft ground, extension rims with lugs could be bolted on. The Avery could work in the field at 2 mph (3.2 kph) or trundle along a hard road at 15 mph (24 kph).

It's not a new idea—1910 Avery.

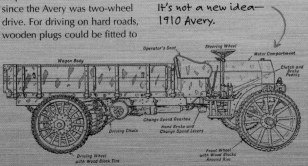

PICKUP TRACTOR-TRUCKS

The 1950s Dodge Power Wagon was originally designed as a standard pickup, but the factory four-wheel-drive option meant it was also marketed as a tractor. It was taken seriously enough to go in 1950 to the University of Nebraska, where all agricultural tractors sold in the United States had to be tested, undergoing all the official tests just like any other tractor. It did well, although the testers added over 2,000 pounds (907 kg) of iron ballast to the rear wheels, and nearly 1,200 pounds (544 kg) to the fronts, to help it along. It managed to lug a maximum pull of 6,408 pounds (2,906 kg) in low gear, thanks in part to a two-range eight-speed transmission that covered 2 to 54 mph (3.2 to 87 kph).

The most successful tractor-truck of all was, and continues to be, the Mercedes Unimog. Launched in the late 1940s, it came with a power takeoff and two hydraulic linkages (one front, one back), plus a belt pulley. Its four-wheel drive, equal-sized wheels, and multirange transmission made it OK with light field work as well as road hauling at speeds up to 31 mph (50 kph). A Unimog could not plow in tricky soil, but it could seed or spread fertilizer, carrying supplies on its load bed. The original 25 hp Unimog has evolved into a far more sophisticated machine of up to 200 hp, with more emphasis on the transport role, since in modern times only 10 percent of buyers are farmers.

It sure doesn't look like a tractor.

THE JEEP TRACTOR

Was the Jeep ever a tractor? It certainly was. After World War II, Willys-Overland was looking for new markets for the Jeep, and the company decided to market it as an all-around farm vehicle. Among the later options was a three-point hitch and hydraulic lift. It was never intended to replace the tractor, but rather was meant to be used as an adaptable farm vehicle that could take on light field work. The English Land Rover could be used in the same way.

Could this really cultivate a field?

Front End Loaders

A front end loader turns the average farm tractor into a handy lift-and-carry machine for use around the yard. A loader consists of two heavy-duty arms, pivoted at the lower end of a frame attached centrally in the tractor's wheelbase. Oil from the hydraulic system is pumped to a ram on each side of the tractor to raise the loader. It's lowered by its own weight, which forces oil back into the hydraulic system.

Loaders are very adaptable and can carry a manure fork, grain bucket, silage grab, bale handler, or pallet fork. A typical loader-equipped 55 hp tractor can lift 1.1 ton (1 tonne) about 9.8 feet (3 m); a 120 hp tractor can lift 2.2 tons (2 tonnes) about 13 feet (4 m).

How Much Tractor Noise Is Safe?

Maximum safe exposure time (OSHA limits, 1978)

SOUND LEVEL DB(A)	TIME PERMITTED (HRS-MINS)
85	16-0
90	8-0
95	4-0
100	2-0
105	1-0
110	0-30
115	0-15
116+	None

Tote that bale.

MODEL T TRACTORS

For farmers who couldn't afford a real tractor, or a second one, a number of companies offered conversions of the Ford Model T. By the late 1920s, just about every American farm had a Model T somewhere.

A typical example was the Feeny, which replaced the Tin Lizzie's rear end with an extended chassis and bigger wheels driven by internal gears. Final drive was by spur pinions mounted on the ends of the standard rear axle and meshing with the wheel gears.

Model T tractors weren't as capable as true farm machines, but they were useful for light jobs, and far cheaper. And there was lots of choice—in 1919, forty-five different T conversions were listed.

Not a Model T but is it a car or tractor?

SNOWBLOWING

Tractors are especially well suited for snowblower operation. Snowblowers clear roads, railways, and airport runways by scooping up the snow and blowing it away from the cleared area. Four-wheel-drive tractors can cope with snow, and they have the surplus engine power and power takeoff to drive the blower itself. Of tractor manufacturers, Allis-Chalmers once made stand-alone snowblowers, and John Deere still does.

I'm blown away by this.

The Retro Tractor

Nostalgia, as the saying goes, isn't what it used to be. That's a good joke, but it's not true. Today we can buy clothes, furniture, even houses, in a nostalgic retro style that harks back to a previous age. Cars, shoes, kitchen appliances, and music can all be had in retro form. And, in early 2009, tractors followed suit.

The New Holland Boomer 8N is an unabashed evocation of the original Ford 8N of 1947. The same rounded bonnet, grille, and headlights. The same red and cream color scheme. Even the seat is styled to look like the old steel pan, even though it's well padded and fully adjustable.

Of course, under its retro skin the twenty-first century 8N is a thoroughly modern tractor, with power steering, good brakes, and a CVT automatic transmission. But it evokes the 1940s with style.

Like a twenty-something in a tweed suit.

Twisted Belts

C'mon, let's twist again.

Ever wondered why the belt drive from an old tractor, usually driving a thresher, is twisted 180 degrees?

It's not this way in order to keep the belt on the pulleys, as is often assumed. The shape is called a Mobius Band, and it ensures that both sides of the belt are being worn. If this seems difficult to visualize, make up a "belt" out of a strip of paper, twist it like a thresher drive belt, and run your finger along its entire length—your finger will touch the whole of the belt, not just one side.

The same principle was used on old-fashioned typewriters, to wear the ribbon evenly, and on tape recorders, where a twisted tape lasted twice as long as a straight one.

WHAT DOES THAT MEAN?

Rule of three.

Three-Point Hitch

The three-point hitch, or hydraulic linkage, was Harry Ferguson's great legacy to the farm tractor and probably the greatest leap forward ever in tractor design. It's now almost universal on farm tractors. Before Harry perfected his idea, implements were attached to the tractor by a simple drawbar. This unfortunately allowed plows to bog down and cause the tractor to rear up, and many drivers were killed in this way. Ferguson's answer was to attach the plow at three points—two to haul it and a top link to provide automatic draft control via hydraulics. If the plow hit a sticky patch, the hydraulics automatically raised it enough to prevent it from getting bogged down. The hydraulics also allow for easy raising and lowering of implements.

Tractor Cross

★ Tractor cross, a race around a bumpy dirt track, is a popular sport in France, and the first event there was held at Le Mans in 1996. Two years later, the French set up a full championship, with twenty-eight teams competing for the title. There were two classes: up to 50 hp, and 50 hp and over.

★ Tractor cross can involve heavy modifications, with higher gearing and smaller rear wheels to boost speed to over 45 mph (72 kph), while the smaller wheels also make the tractor less likely to tip over in corners. Still, they all have to be fitted with a substantial roll cage, just in case.

★ Engines are tuned to rev to two or three times faster than a standard tractor engine—up to 4,000 rpm. Some racers add suspension as well—coil springs or even hydropneumatics. Three- and four-cylinder engines are allowed in tractor cross races, up to 305 cubic inches (5 L), but no turbos, and no four-wheel drive. And, because this is France, drivers have to sprint across to their machines at the start, in true Le Mans 24-hour style.

Forget Formula One. Real men race tractors.

HARRY FERGUSON

Most Important Tractor: FERGUSON MODEL A

Like Henry Ford, Harry Ferguson was a farmer's son, though he hailed from Ireland. Also like Henry, he could be difficult and irascible, so maybe it was no coincidence that he fell out with three key business partners—David Brown, Henry Ford, and Massey-Harris. And, just like Henry, Ferguson was an exceptional engineer with a commercial head on his shoulders who broke new ground in tractor design.

The Three-Point Hitch: Ferguson's Legacy
As a young man, he was more interested in planes and racing cars, but, after becoming the Belfast agent for the American-made Overtime tractor, he turned his inventive mind to improving the standard implement hitch. The famous three-point hitch was the result, and it really did change the tractor industry. Ferguson went on to make his equally famous handshake agreement with Henry Ford that eventually ended in court. Harry Ferguson sold his tractor business to Massey-Harris and went on to design four-wheel-drive cars. He died in 1960.

CARTOON TRACTORS
Farm tractors are a favorite subject for cartoonists. And why not? Big, chunky tires and bright colors are a gift to them, like a politician with a distinctive face. Besides that, the driver is in full view, so that's another image to play with. In children's cartoons, tractors are naturally given smiley faces and cheery personalities; the farm tractor is everyone's friend.

BEFORE CATERPILLAR

When archrivals Holt and Best merged to form Caterpillar in 1925, various folks had been experimenting with tracklayers for the better part of a century. This quaint device came complete with a tiller wheel that looks to be straight off a four-masted schooner. Designed by Boydell, this tracklaying steamer was actually used by the British army during the Crimean War in 1854. Evidently, the army decision-makers weren't impressed, for sixty years later the British War Office turned down the Hornsby-Akroyd crawler tractor. For a little while longer, they relied on horses to haul their heavy guns.

The top brass weren't impressed with this.

Three wheels on my wagon and I'm still rollin' along.

Tricycle Tractors

The "row-crop tractor" was one of the standard classes of machine in the United States from the 1920s up to the 1960s, when the term faded away. Designed to work with crops grown in rows, such as cotton and corn, it often had adjustable treads (width between the wheels) for working with rows of different spacings.

An alternative to an adjustable front axle, and one that quickly found favor in the 1930s, was the tricycle format, with a single or twin front wheel mounted on a single pivot. Although it was not as stable as a true four-wheel tractor, doing away with the front axle made row-crop work much easier, as the front wheel simply rolled down the gap between rows. The rear axle was usually still width-adjustable.

Tricycle tractors remained mostly confined to North America, and here too the format faded out in the 1960s, as the distinction between row-crop and standard tread tractors became increasingly meaningless. Today, the tricycle tractor is no more.

HOURS, NOT MILES

A tractor's life isn't measured in miles, like a car's, but in the hours it's worked—this is a better indication of how hard it's been run. In an hour's plowing, a tractor might only cover a couple of miles, but in that hour it's worked far harder than it would if it had hauled an empty trailer on the road for an hour. So if you're looking at a secondhand tractor, don't ask how many miles it's traveled; instead, ask how many hours it's worked—one thousand hours a year is a good average.

Quieter Cabs

Modern tractor cabs are carefully designed to reduce noise, so that operators' hearing isn't damaged by the high decibels produced by tractor engines. But it wasn't always like this. Back in the 1960s, as tractor power increased year after year, researchers were puzzled that, in practice, the latest, most powerful tractors weren't boosting productivity as expected.

The reason was simple: at full power, a tractor engine produced an unbearable amount of noise in the cab, and drivers were holding back to save their eardrums! The University of Nebraska conducted a noise test from 1971 and the following year John Deere launched Sound-Gard, the new quieter cab on its Generation II tractors. It even came with the option of a stereo radio!

In 1975 Allis-Chalmers responded with its Acousta Cab. This was carefully designed with nonparallel surfaces, rubber isolation mounts, flexible control cables, fiberglass insulation, and foam padding. Finally, farmers' hearing stood a chance of lasting into their twilight years.

LUGS AND SPADES

In the early days, manufacturers tried all manner of wheel lugs and spades in an attempt to improve traction while minimizing damage to the soil. Avery offered five alternatives: three were designed for heavier soils, No. 4 "Never Slip" was for soft ground, and No. 5 "Perfection Lugs" was for sand and light, loose soil. Another manufacturer tried casting lugs patterned like the foot of a mastodon.

Or, how about this ingenious device? The spades are mounted eccentrically so that they enter and withdraw from the ground vertically, without packing the soil.

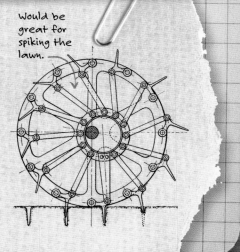

What horsepower am I?

THE HORSEPOWER JUNGLE

Tractor power is traditionally measured in horsepower (hp), but what do all those abbreviations mean? And how much is 1 hp?

- **1 hp** – 33,000 pound-feet/minute or 745.7 watts

- **SAE hp** – Society of Automotive Engineers (USA)—gross, net, or (since 2005) certified

- **DIN hp** – German standard DIN 70020. Also known as PS

- **ECE hp** – EU standard, similar to DIN

- **ISO 14396** – New ISO standard for all nonroad engines

- **watts** – Gradually replacing horsepower as the standard measure of engine power in Europe

Why Are Old Tractors Left To Rot?

Old cars and trucks get sent to the scrap yard, but, like a retired draught horse put out to grass, old tractors stay on the farm.

Why?

❖ Farmers have the space to keep old machinery. So why waste time and money hauling the tractor to a scrap yard miles away?

❖ Old tractors are a useful source of spare parts.

❖ And, let's face it—it's hard to see a faithful old machine that has served you for twenty-odd years banished to the crusher.

Old tractors never die...

These boots were made for rolling.

WHY ARE TRACTOR TIRES SO CHUNKY?

Tractors depend on their tires for traction in sticky conditions, and the big rubber lugs are designed to push against the ground without slipping, however muddy or rocky it is. All would come to a halt if the space between the lugs clogged with mud, though, so they are designed to be self-cleaning, the tractor's movement squeezing mud out between the lugs and allowing it to fall to the ground.

MILESTONE TRACTORS

INTERNATIONAL FARMALL

DATES: 1924–1932

WHY IS IT IMPORTANT? THIS IS THE FIRST DO-IT-ALL TRACTOR.

ENGINE TYPE: WATER-COOLED, FOUR-CYLINDER, 221 CI (3.6 L)

POWER: 13/20 HP

WEIGHT: 3,650 POUNDS (1650 KG)

PRICE: $950/£578 (APPROXIMATELY $11,982/£7,285 TODAY)

GOOD POINTS: VERY ADAPTABLE.

BAD POINTS: VERY FEW.

RANDOM FACT: INTERNATIONAL HARVESTER ENGINEERS ALSO CONSIDERED BUILDING A MODERN STEAM TRACTOR; FORTUNATELY, THEY CHOSE THE FARMALL.

HISTORY: International's Farmall defined the American row crop tractor, but it was a lot more than that. As the name suggests, this was the first tractor that really could do everything. Until the Farmall came along, tractors were either big, heavy, and powerful for belt work, powering threshers and the like, or they were light, spindly "motor plows" that could work row crops. Even the Fordson, for example, was too clumsy to cultivate weeds out of cotton or maize rows. The Farmall was different. At 18 hp (which was soon upped to 20 hp) it was strong enough to power a thresher or haul a plow. It was also lightweight and nimble enough to do delicate row crop work without damaging the crop. The Farmall could turn as tight as you like, and it had a high chassis to skim over the top of the crop. From his high seat, the driver had fine visibility of a mid-mounted cultivation tool.

Strangely, International Harvester was hesitant about introducing the Farmall, thinking it would steal sales from the conventional 10-20. But once it was on the market, the floodgates opened—over four thousand Farmalls were sold in 1926, and forty thousand in 1930. So resonant was the Farmall name that it was used by International Harvester into the 1960s—a true milestone.

THE FARMALL REALLY COULD FARM IT ALL.

Case Quadtrac

The Case Quadtrac was, and remains, unique—it's the only tractor to combine crawler tracks with a pivot-steer chassis.

Certainly, the rubber-tracked Caterpillar Challenger caused quite a stir in the world of tractors—here was a completely new idea that promised all the advantages of a conventional crawler, with longer-lasting, road-friendly rubber tracks. In addition, the John Deere company lost no time in coming up with its own rubber-tracked tractors, but, like the Challenger, they had rigid chassis.

The Four-Track Idea

The Case-Steiger engineers took a different approach. Instead of two large tracks, they thought, why not use four smaller ones on an existing pivot-steer chassis? Crawlers with two tracks turn by slowing or stopping the inside track, which is inefficient and leads to skidding and scuffing. On the Case, however, all four tracks were powered throughout, which made for cleaner, more efficient turns. Each track put 9.8 feet (3 m) of rubber on the ground, and Case claimed a ground pressure of just 5.3 psi (0.37 bar) despite an all-up weight of 20 tons (18 tonnes). Good weight distribution reduced the need for balance weights and added up to excellent traction—the Quadtrac could haul a ten-furrow plow in very sticky conditions with only 2 percent wheel slip.

TOP TIPS
Refuel at the end of each day, not in the morning—a nearly empty tank will allow moist air to accumulate.

Are you looking at my tracks?

Muscle Before Tractors

For thousands of years, animal muscle—from horses, oxen, mules, and sometimes donkeys—was the primary motive power on farms. They did everything: plowing, hauling, and powering machinery to thresh the grain and prepare feed for livestock. It was a hard life for both the animal and the farm worker, and some animals were literally worked to death. Harry Ferguson, always keen to point out the advantages of tractors, said that a horse needed 5 acres (2 hectares) of land a year just to keep it fed—land that could be growing productive, saleable crops.

> I wish they'd hurry up and invent the tractor.

THE BIGGEST TRACTOR FACTORY

Minsk Tractor Works, in the former Soviet Union, is surely the biggest tractor factory in the world. It's actually a collection of eleven huge plants that between them employ nearly thirty thousand people.

Since opening for business in May 1946, this Russian giant has churned out three million tractors, half a million of which have been exported. (The fact that the home USSR market swallowed 2.5 million machines says something about its own massive size). Despite the collapse of the Eastern Bloc, Minsk is still a major tractor producer, and the company claims to account for 8 percent of the world's entire production. It currently offers a lineup of sixty-two different models, from 35 hp compacts to 300 hp supertractors, with specials for cotton, rice, and horticulture in between.

> "I'VE GOT A BRAND-NEW COMBINE HARVESTER"
> Artist: The Wurzels
> Album: The Finest 'Arvest of the Wurzels (1976)
> What's the Story?
> A farmer makes a proposal—her land and his combine harvester. Who could refuse?

Fresh out of Minsk, one of the three million.

Prairie Monsters

In the early days, the assumption was bigger was always better.

When some of North America's prairies were being plowed up for the first time, giant tractors were needed to do the job, taking over from the big steam traction engines. Emerson-Brantingham's four-cylinder Big Four was typical, and could pull a ten-furrow plow. Forward vision was tricky on the Big Fours, so they were provided with a forward outrigger wheel and arrow, to give the driver a better idea of which way the front wheels were pointing.

Size Matters

In those days (before the Fordson and other, more manageable tractors came along), the general assumption was that bigger would always be better. Twin City's 60-90 was one such large tractor, measuring 21 feet (6.4 m) in length. It carried 95 gallons (359.6 L) of fuel, 116 gallons (439.1 L) of cooling water, and made up a shipping weight of 28,000 pounds (11,793 kg). And, unlike some, it was guaranteed to deliver its rated horsepower.

Advance Rumeley's OilPull was certainly in the "bigger is better" category. The company's most famous stunt, in 1911, was to link three of these giants together and pull a row of fifty plow shares—that's fifty furrows in one pass. Not bad.

Elegant Tractor Style

The 1930s was the age of streamlining. Cars, trucks, even refrigerators and toasters took on a new streamlined elegance that suggested a modern age of speed and luxury. And tractors were no exception, at least in the United States (it took the Europeans a little while to catch up).

Bring in the Designers
International Harvester called in renowned designer Raymond Loewy to spruce up its tractors, and he did an excellent job, enclosing the fuel tank, steering rod, and radiator into a single rounded housing. Loewy even redesigned the wheels to give an impression of strength with lightness.

John Deere did the same in 1939, and their stylist of choice was Henry Dreyfuss. He rounded off some of Johnny Popper's sharp edges but left the tractors with a straightforward, no-nonsense look. By contrast, Oliver did the job in-house, and the work was arguably just as good as that of the big-name stylists. The six-cylinder 70 looked especially elegant, slim, and streamlined, with a tilted-back radiator that suggested speed. If there is such a thing as a beautiful tractor, this is it.

1930s elegance, in a tractor.

Cage wheels spread the weight.

CAGE WHEELS

Cage wheels are a means of maintaining traction when the way gets extremely wet and boggy, such as in rice paddies. The idea is exactly the same as with any other large tire or crawler track—to spread the tractor's weight over as large an area as possible, reducing ground pressure and preventing the tractor from sinking. In less extreme conditions, narrower cage discs can be bolted onto conventional wheels and tires to give extra flotation.

beautiful? Fendt showed this "Black Beauty" as a concept in 2007. Not only did it win two design awards, but the public reaction was so enthusiastic that Fendt decided to offer something similar to tractor buyers.

The "Design Line" option pack came with a chrome bonnet head, stainless steel exhaust, Dieselross steering wheel, and a custom paint job in black and red, steel blue, pine green, or, of course, plain black.

MODEL TRACTORS

Small tractors are big business. It's not just children who buy toy tractors these days. Adult collectors can spend $300/£182 or more on incredibly detailed 1:16 models that are meant to be admired, not pushed along the carpet or (worse still) outside on the lawn. Companies like Ertl, Britains, and Wiking offer a vast range of model tractors, from cheap 1:64 items that will keep Junior happy on a Sunday morning, to rare limited editions. The best models are fully licensed from the maker of the real thing, designed using CAD, and built from laser-cut steel. But there are still plenty of cheaper models, just right for pocket-money budgets.

Don't Throw It Away!
Older models are becoming collectors' items too. Do you still have the Dinky, Spot-On, or Triang model tractor you played with as a kid? It might be worth more than you think. But only if it's in good condition with the original box!

Perfect for carpet farmers.

BARBECUE FUEL FOR TRACTORS?

Gasoline and diesel became scarce during World War II, but tractors had to keep working, and one alternative was to convert to producer gas. A charcoal burner mounted on the front burned wood chips, which produced the gas.

Twin wheels get more done.

Twin Wheels

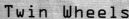

WHAT DOES THAT MEAN?

For a tractor, traction is everything, and sometimes a standard set of tires, however big and chunky, simply can't provide enough grip. The answer since the 1960s has been to use twin wheels, doubling the amount of rubber on the field and dramatically improving traction. When that isn't enough, triple wheels are sometimes put on big supertractors. Why not simply add bigger single tires? Twins and triples are far more adaptable and can be removed when not needed. Also, massively wide single tires would be more expensive, generate more friction on tarmac, and be less maneuverable.

Have I done an acre yet?

WHAT IS AN ACRE?

The origins of the acre lie in the strength of the average draft horse. A typical team of oxen or horses hauling a plow could manage to cover around 220 yards (201 m) before needing to stop for a rest. So fields were usually cultivated in strips 220 yards (a furlong) in length. Strips were traditionally one-tenth of a furlong (22 yards, or 20 m, a chain) wide and the area of the strip (220 by 22 yards, or 201 by 20 m) was one acre.

POWER LOSSES

Not all of a tractor's power makes it through to the wheels or drawbar. Power is lost through rolling resistance, wheel slip, the transmission, and tire flex. So a 100 hp tractor (that's 100 hp at the engine flywheel) delivers only around 85 hp at the PTO, and at the drawbar it delivers just 60 hp (on firm soil), 50 hp (on tilled soil), or 45 hp (on soft soil).

DE-STONING

Rocky, stony soil is difficult to cultivate, so farmers sometimes use a machine that takes stones out. Trailing behind the tractor, it lifts the previously farmed layer, sifts out the stones and clods, and returns soil to the ground in a shaped bed ready for seeding. Depending on the size of the machine, it produces a stone-free path 4.9 to 6.5 feet (1.5 to 2 m) wide.

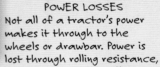

Not all that power reaches the plow.

What do you mean, I've got to do field work too?

ROAD HAULERS

Research at the University of Manchester in 1972 found that modern tractors spent up to 70 percent of their time on the road, often hauling trailers. Ever-larger farms mean that the percentage in the early twenty-first century is probably even higher.

Interestingly, researchers also found that tractors saw even more road use in Turkey and India. The explanation was simple—the tractor was often the only motorized transport owned by a farming family, so it would be used for all sorts of road jobs, from collecting fertilizer to taking the whole family into town.

"SHE THINKS MY TRACTOR'S SEXY"
Artist: Kenny Chesney
Album: Everywhere We Go (1999)
What's the Story?
Are tractors sexy? They are in this song.

MILESTONE TRACTORS

JOHN DEERE MODEL R

DATES: 1949–1955

WHY IS IT IMPORTANT? FIRST SUCCESSFUL DIESEL WHEELED
TRACTOR IN THE UNITED STATES.

ENGINE TYPE: WATER-COOLED, TWIN-CYLINDER, 416 CI (6.5 L)

POWER: 51 HP

WEIGHT: 7,603 POUNDS (3.45 KG)

PRICE: $3,650/£2,219 IN 1954 (APPROXIMATELY $29,267/£17,788 TODAY)

GOOD POINTS: UNRIVALED FUEL EFFICIENCY.

BAD POINTS: COMPLICATED COLD-START ARRANGEMENTS.

RANDOM FACT: THE MODEL R HAD TWO ENGINES: A BIG DIESEL, AND A
VERY SMALL GASOLINE DONKEY TO PRE-WARM THE MAIN UNIT
UP ON COLD MORNINGS.

HISTORY: By the late 1940s, there was nothing new about diesels. German, French and British tractors had been using them through the 1930s, and Caterpillar built a whole range of diesel-powered crawlers. But until the John Deere R came along, there was no American-made wheeled tractor with a diesel engine.

This mattered, because through the 1930s, as US tractors got ever bigger and more powerful, they also turned into gas guzzlers. John Deere realized this and started work on a diesel that would give plenty of power but sip rather than guzzle fuel.

The result was the Model R, which stuck to Johnny Popper's twin-cylinder layout, though in massive 416 ci form. With 51 hp at the PTO, it was the most powerful tractor Deere had ever made—it could haul a five-furrow plow with ease. And it really was efficient, setting a new fuel economy record at Nebraska that wasn't bettered for several years—its fuel efficiency is still better than many tractors built in the 1970s and 1980s.

HUNKY, CHUNKY, AND EFFICIENT—THE JOHN DEERE MODEL R.

Here's faithful old Dobbin...and a couple of horses.

Tractors And Horses, Side By Side

Here's the theoretical history of tractor versus horse in a nutshell: Horse power (of the four-legged kind) rules the farm for hundreds of years. Then tractors come along and millions of horses are put out of a job, retired to grazing if they're lucky, sold off to the abattoir if not.

Except it didn't happen quite like that, at least not in North America, and not at first, anyway. In 1909, there were a mere two thousand tractors working on American farms, and a staggering twenty-five million horses and mules. A decade later, in 1920, there were over two hundred thousand tractors out there working the fields—but the number of horses and mules had actually increased, to over twenty-six million.

So Why Did Farmers Hang on to Their Horses?

★ **Suspicion:** Early farmers were understandably suspicious of the new tractor technology, unwilling to ditch immediately the actual horse power that had served them so well.

★ **Convenience:** The first tractors weren't convenient push-button machines, so for light jobs it was simply easier to put a horse or two in harness.

★ **Equipment:** Farmers still owned a whole range of horse-drawn equipment, with years of life left in it, so to scrap all of that would have meant money down the drain.

★ **Money:** A tractor was a big investment. Most farmers could only afford to buy one, so they kept the horses to supplement it.

★ **Transport:** Until farms could afford to buy a Model T as well as a tractor, the horse and buggy was the quickest way to get to town.

★ **Emotion:** You don't get rid of faithful servants just like that.

Turbocharger

WHAT DOESTHAT MEAN?

Turbocharging is a means of forcing extra air into an engine, which can be mixed with extra fuel in order to produce more power. Turbos came to tractors in the early 1960s, when a power race was underway and all the companies wanted to have the most powerful tractor on the market. The simplest way to increase engine power is to install a bigger unit, but ever-bigger engines are also heavier and more cumbersome than smaller ones. The answer was turbocharging, which in the case of the pioneering Allis-Chalmers D19 boosted power by 25 percent. Turbos are especially well suited to diesel engines, which is why they swiftly became a favorite for increasing tractor power.

Well blow me down.

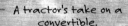

A tractor's take on a convertible.

SUN SHADE

Tractor cabs aren't just there to keep rain off; in the days before air-conditioned cabs, many tractors heading for hot, sunny climates were fitted with sun shades. Some sold in Third World markets still are. A tractor driver out in the open for ten to twelve hours at a time is vulnerable to sunstroke, and there are few places less shady than the top of an open tractor on a hot, sunny day.

WHERE ARE TRACTORS MADE?

Around 220 companies currently build tractors. Here's a list of where they come from:

Argentina	Hungary	Russia	Uganda
Austria	India	Serbia	UK
Belarus	Iran	Slovenia	Ukraine
Brazil	Italy	South Africa	Uruguay
China	Japan	South Korea	USA
Czech Republic	Kurdistan	Spain	Uzbekistan
Denmark	Libya	Sudan	Venezuela
Finland	Moldovia	Switzerland	Vietnam
France	Pakistan	Syria	Zimbabwe
Georgia	Poland	Tajikistan	
Germany	Romania	Thailand	

THE FIRST JAPANESE APPEARS

The first Japanese tractors to enter the American market were from Kubota, launched in 1965. Neither of them—the 9 hp gasoline Kubota RV and the 20 hp diesel D20—was in the Steiger class. However, Kubota would become a leading manufacturer in the compact and garden tractor market and later exported full-size machines as well.

It wasn't just cameras and motorcycles.

Cable Plowing

With cable plowing or cultivating, two steam traction engines with winding drums were placed at either side of the field, and the implement was dragged to and fro between them by cable. It sounds like two machines doing the work of one, but there was a good reason. Heavy steam engines didn't have the traction to direct haul a plow, and their immense weight meant they were very prone to bogging down. This wasn't such a problem on the dryer soils of North America, but in Europe cable plowing was popular on large farms from the 1850s onward. As you might imagine, cable plowing called for good coordination between the operators of the two engines, who, when parked on either side of a rise, might not be able to see each other. Communication was often done by whistle.

Cable plowing was popular on heavier European soils.

WHAT DOES THAT MEAN?

Governor

Tractor engines often need to run at a constant speed, either to operate machinery or to maintain a steady pace in the field. The governor does its best to keep engine speed constant, increasing or decreasing fuel delivery as needed for the load. Early governors fitted to tractors, just as on steam traction engines, were centrifugal devices, but modern tractors use electronic control to maintain that constant engine speed.

Going steady—governor kept things even.

FÜR SAAT UND ERNTE

F 15

Fendt Dieselross

=FENDT=

Dieselross

Rotaped

There are crawlers, and then there are crawlers. The Rotapeds were invented in England during World War II and offered as a conversion for Fordsons and the International B250 right up to 1967. Six flat pans replaced each wheel, the idea being to spread the tractor's weight and reduce the chances of it sinking into the soil. The makers claimed that they exerted only 7 pounds (3.175 kg) per square inch (6.45 sq cm) apiece.

How did they work?
The pans were held in place and hauled around by a system of chains, and each set of six was a direct replacement for a conventional wheel. The tractor's rear axle remained in place, and steering was done by the front wheels, which were extended and filled with concrete to counteract the extra rearward weight of the Rotapeds. The makers also claimed that a wheeled tractor could be converted to Rotapeds in just thirty minutes, though that might have been a little optimistic.

Rotapeds actually worked, proving useful for plowing in soft, wet soil. They were particularly useful for trench digging and were often used along with a Howard trencher, which was reckoned to dig 175 yards (160 m) an hour.

HORSEPOWER ACROSS THE WORLD

Most countries measure horsepower in similar ways, but not all call it by the same name.

- Germany – PS (*Pferdestake* = "horse strength")
- France – ch or cv (not to be confused with CV, a taxation measure of horsepower)
- Italy – *Cavalli* (CV)
- Spain – *Caballos* (CV)
- Portugal – *Cavalos* (CV)
- Holland – *Paardnkracht* (pk)
- Sweden – *Hostkaft* (hk)
- Finland – *Hevosvoima* (hv)
- Norway/Denmark – *Hestekraft* (hk)
- Hungary – *Loero* (HE)
- Czech Republic/Slovakia – *Konske sila* (k or ks)
- Serbia/Croatia – *Konjskasnaga* (k or ks)

If it moves, somebody somewhere will race it.

Tractor Racing

Believe it or not, people really do race tractors, gearing them up to reach much higher speeds than standard. The usual venue is a makeshift dirt track. In India, tractor racing is part of the Punjab's annual rural Olympics (along with bullock cart racing and balancing a bicycle on the chin). It's popular in Russia, too—at one meeting in the southern Rostov region, fifteen thousand spectators watched a tractor race as well as a tractor tug-of-war.

In the United States, a celebrity tractor race was held at the 2009 Country Music Association's annual festival in Nashville. It wasn't a high-speed event, though—competitors had to drive a compact New Holland through an obstacle course of traffic cones.

The Origins of Tractor Racing

Tractor racing isn't a new idea. Allis-Chalmers hit on it as a means of publicizing the pneumatic rubber tire option on the new Model U. The company geared the tractors up for higher speeds and hired celebrity racing drivers like Barney Oldfield and Ab Jenkins to tour the United States during 1933, keeping the crowds entertained at county fairs.

MARRIED ON A TRACTOR

Many a tractor has been used to transport a bride and groom away from the church after the marriage ceremony. Greg Norroth and his bride, Barbara, of Antioch, Illinois, actually got married on a pair of IH Farmalls; the minister and happy couple were supported by a platform resting on the pair of tractors.

TOP TIPS

When traversing slopes, watch out for dips on the low side, and bumps on the high side.

MOWING

Grass mowers come in many shapes and sizes, but with a machine above a certain size it's simply more economical to use a standard tractor with a mower attachment. In the past, mowers were traditionally side-mounted and hinged upright for transport. Now they are increasingly front-mounted and powered by a front PTO. Tractors used exclusively for this work will often have grass tires, which have a less-aggressive tread than farm tractor tires.

Beats the hell out of a pair of shears.

Old Abe

Old Abe, an eagle, was the trademark of J. I. Case for more than one hundred years. He really did exist, and was bought by the Eighth Wisconsin Infantry's Company C from a local farmer, for just $2.50/£1.51. Old Abe became the Company's mascot and accompanied them into battle many times in the early 1860s. They named him after President Abraham Lincoln, and the eagle became a legend, often losing feathers to enemy bullets. He was so respected that even General Ulysses S. Grant would doff his hat as he passed.

The military eagle retired in 1864, but that wasn't the end of his career as a mascot. Jerome Case, founder of J. I. Case, was so impressed by the sight of Old Abe next to his military colors that he adopted his likeness for the company logo. Old Abe perched on a globe, with the slogan "The Sign of Mechanical Excellence the World Over," became inextricably linked with Case tractors.

So strong was the association that when the board suggested in 1956 that Old Abe be discarded in favor of something more modern, the longstanding chairman Leon Clausmann rose up out of his seat in anger. Only after Clausmann died nearly ten years later was Old Abe finally retired in favor of a new logo.

Old Abe was also the mascot for:
☆ US Army 101st Airborne Division
☆ Eau Claire Memorial High School
☆ Racine Case High School

Old Abe was a real eagle.

MILESTONE TRACTORS

FARMALL SUPER MTA

DATES: 1952–1954

WHY IS IT IMPORTANT? IT PIONEERED DUAL-RANGE ON-THE-GO SHIFTING.

ENGINE TYPE: WATER-COOLED, FOUR-CYLINDER, 264 CI (4.3 L)

POWER: 33/41 HP

WEIGHT: 5,725 POUNDS (2,597 KG)

PRICE: $2,925/£1,778 (APPROXIMATELY $23,807/£14,472 TODAY)

GOOD POINTS: ON-THE-GO SHIFTING AND TEN FORWARD SPEEDS.

BAD POINTS: THE COMPETITION SOON CAUGHT UP.

RANDOM FACT: THE MTA ABANDONED THE "FARMALL" RADIATOR BADGE FOR INTERNATIONAL HARVESTER'S NEW CORPORATE LOGO.

HISTORY: Transmission design is crucial to tractors, perhaps even more so than the design of the engine. A useful tractor has to give usable power over a wide range of speeds, from slow walking in the fields to fast hauling on the road.

By the early 1950s, tractor transmissions had progressed from two, to four or five speeds, but you still had to stop to change gears. Do that in a sticky patch while plowing, and you might not get started again. So what was desperately needed was more ratios, and a means of shifting on the go. The Farmall Super MTA answered both needs.

Based on the aging Farmall M, the Farmall Super MTA offered the new feature, the "Torque Amplifier." This was a two-speed planetary transmission mounted in front of the standard five-speed gearbox. So it gave two ranges and doubled the number of forward ratios to ten. Better still, you could shift between the two ranges without declutching or stopping. This was the embryo of the modern power-shift transmission, and, though the opposition soon caught up, International Harvester got there first. It sold twenty-two thousand MTAs in three years.

SHIFT ON THE GO, A NEW IDEA IN 1952.

Massey-Ferguson 1200:
The European-American

The classic big supertractor—with four-wheel drive, pivot-steer chassis, large powerful diesel engine—was designed specifically for the wide open spaces of the United States and Canada. Steiger, Versatile, and Big Bud were all built in North America as well. In the USSR, Belarus tractors followed the same format.

But the Massey-Ferguson 1200 was different: it had all the same attributes as the traditional supertractors, but on a smaller scale, and it was made in Britain, not the United States.

A Scaled-Down Supertractor
Instead of a massive six-cylinder or V8 diesel, the 1200 (launched in 1971) used a more modest Perkins diesel engine of 354 cubic inches (5.8 L) and 91 hp at the PTO. But it still had four-wheel drive through equal-sized wheels, and perfect 50/50 weight distribution. At the time, it was the only standard production four-wheel-drive tractor offered at an affordable price. The 1200 sold well throughout Europe and was soon upgraded as the 96 hp 1250. Of course, it was soon overtaken in the outright power race, but its fine traction and maneuverability made it a farmers' favorite until it was dropped in 1982.

TOP TIPS
Make sure no one is near the tractor when moving off, lowering an implement, or engaging the PTO.

TRACTOR DOWNTIME

With all their downtime, tractors may spend only a little more than half the available working hours on productive work. This is how the average tractor spends its working time.

Productive work	55 percent
Rainy days and illness	15 percent
Holidays	8 percent
Travel	12.5 percent
Maintenance/breaks/briefings	7.5 percent
Breakdowns/mishaps	2 percent

Source: Farm Contractor & Large Scale Farmer

Relax guys, maintenance and breakdowns are less than 10 percent.

> "That's the great thing about a tractor. You can't really hear the phone ring."
>
> JEFF FOXWORTHY

Three Wheels Good?

The designers of the Victor tractor of 1919 (right) weren't afraid of lateral thinking or radical design. Their machine had two huge front wheels, which transmitted power from engine to ground. So big were they that the tractor's four-cylinder engine was mounted inside them, driving through an internal gear on each wheel. The Victor had two speeds (2.3 and 3.2 mph, or 3.7 kph and 5.1 kph), and its tiny single rear wheel did the steering.

Life saver—Talus can wade through water 8 feet (2.5m) deep, and park in 30 feet (9m).

Lifeboat Tractor

In the United Kingdom, the Royal National Lifeboat Institution uses specially designed tractors for launching its fleet of lifeboats into the water. A tractor is often the only way to launch at low tide, and a special breed of machine has been developed that can operate in deep water.

Amphibious Tractors

The Talus MB-H is a typical lifeboat launcher, basically a watertight hull on tracks, with all the machinery and equipment installed inside, protected from the saltwater environment. It can tow lifeboat and trailer into water deep enough for launching, and recover the lifeboat by winch. Talus makes both wheeled and tracked machines—the MB-H is tracked, with detachable rubber pads for road work. There's 1.5 feet (0.46 m) of ground clearance, but more impressive is how the tractor can work at full power in up to 8 feet (2.44 m) of water. If it gets into difficulties, it can be battened down and left on the seabed in up to 30 feet (9 m) of water with no ill effects. Power comes from a 210 hp Caterpillar V8, which drives the tractor through a hydrostatic transmission up to 7.5 mph (12 kph).

TALUS MB-H SPECIFICATION

L x W x H	5.48 x 2.44 x 2.97 m
Weight	21 tons (19 tonnes)
Engine type	Caterpillar 3208 V8 diesel
Power	210 bhp
Max revs	2,800 rpm
Transmission	Hydrostatic CVT
Brakes	Hydrostatic fail-safe multi-plate disc
Winch max pull	16.5 tons (15 tonnes)

WORLD'S FIRST V8 TRACTOR

Back in 1915, the Common Sense Gas Tractor Company began building its V8 tractor. The engine measured 317 cubic inches (5.2 L) and offered 20 hp at the drawbar and 40 hp at the belt, both at 1,200 rpm. However, the makers claimed that in emergencies the engine could be revved to produce 70 hp. The V8 came with full pressure oiling, was painted in smart red and yellow, and could be yours for $2,200/£1,336 (approximately $46,982/£28,541 today).

JOHN DEERE

Most Important Tractor:
JOHN DEERE MODEL D

John Deere was a blacksmith, and a mighty good one, who turned one good idea into a phenomenal success story. Based in Vermont, he made his name with high-quality polished hay forks and shovels, but an economic depression forced the young blacksmith to move west in 1836 and try his luck in Illinois. He started out all over again and was soon joined by his growing family.

The Answer to a Sticky Problem
In Illinois, however, the pioneer farmers weren't so happy. The Midwestern soil was fertile, but sticky and heavy, and would cling to a cast-iron plow. Deere's answer was a smooth, highly polished steel plow that would scour itself. It was a huge success, and within ten years his business was making one thousand plows a year.

When Deere died in 1886, his company was making many thousands of plows, cultivators, and other implements every year. It would be over forty years before John Deere's company entered the tractor market, but it stayed and survived, the only major US tractor manufacturer to stay independent through the twentieth century.

Power Takeoff

WHAT DOES THAT MEAN?

The power takeoff shaft—better known as the "PTO"—does exactly what its name describes. It provides a second outlet for engine power, which it uses to drive machinery. PTO-powered machinery includes balers, seeders, and planters, and in each case the engine is powering the machine as well as the tractor itself. Standard PTOs offer two speeds—540 rpm and 1,000 rpm—according to the needs of the machine being driven. The PTO is the modern equivalent of the belt pulley on old tractors, and since the 1950s it has continued to deliver machinery power even when the tractor itself has stopped (which is known as a "live" PTO). International Harvester attempted to replace the PTO in the early 1960s with a front-mounted generator, allowing machinery to use electrical rather than mechanical power, but it never caught on.

Plug-in power.

With a light trailer, he's sipping the fuel.

Which Job Is The Gas Guzzler?

How much fuel does a tractor need for each job? And which uses most? You might think that a tractor storming along the road at speed, towing a trailer, would use more fuel than one working a field at walking pace, but that's not necessarily the case. PTO jobs (powering other machinery) are the most gas-guzzling tasks for a typical tractor, and the most economical is light field work done on half-throttle, such as beet drilling.

Note the difference between the absolute amount of fuel used (gallons per hour) compared to the efficiency of work done (ounces of fuel per kWh)—our typical tractor uses far more fuel on heavy trailer work than light, but it's doing it more efficiently.

JOB	FUEL USE (GALLONS/LITERS PER HOUR)	FUEL EFFICIENCY (OUNCES/GRAMS PER KWH)
Low output	4.8 (18.3)	8.2 (235)
Transport work (light trailer)	5.6 (21.4)	9.7 (275)
High output (e.g., plowing)	9.4 (35.8)	8.1 (230)
PTO work (economy setting)	9.9 (37.5)	8.0 (227)
Top speed range (heavy trailer)	10.2 (38.9)	8.8 (250)
PTO work (standard setting)	11.9 (45.1)	8.0 (227)

(Source: Profi magazine)

WHAT DID WE EVER DO WITHOUT SUSPENSION?

Suspension is now very popular with buyers. In 2009, around half all New Holland T7000s for Europe were ordered with front suspension, and 80 to 90 percent had the optional cab suspension as well.

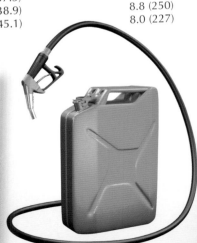

Keeping it on the level: tilting tractors are the answer to hilly country.

Tilting Tractors

Farming in hilly country presents a problem. There's often plenty of productive land on steep hillsides, but these are difficult to cultivate safely, due to the danger that the tractor might tip over. Cultivating up and down the slope, rather than along its side, is one solution, but this is possible only if there's room for a safe headland turn at either end.

Using a tilting tractor is one way around this—allowing the main body of the tractor to keep upright while the axles tilt to suit the slope, to reduce the risk of tipping and to deliver better traction through improved weight distribution. A conventional tractor will have less weight on the "uphill" pair of wheels.

Knudson's Ingenious Idea

The first modern tilting tractor was designed and built in 1974 by Jerome Knudson. Jerome and his father farmed wheat near Crosby, North Dakota, and couldn't find a standard tractor suitable for their hilly terrain.

So Knudson Jr. came up with a self-leveling mechanism that allowed his big four-wheel-drive tractor to traverse steep slopes quite safely. Demand was high among Northwest wheat farmers, and in 1977 Jerome moved production to a new factory. Four Knudson tractors were then offered, at 310 to 360 hp, all powered by an 855 cubic inches (14 L) Cummins power unit. They had a rigid chassis, four-wheel steering, and a cab tall enough for the driver to stand in. The Knudson was an ingenious idea, but it was too specialized to survive, and production ended in 1983.

What Are Carpet Farmers?

Kids who love pushing model tractors across the living room floor.

You should have seen the tractor AFTER he'd tuned it up.

Tractor Pulling Evolves

In the 1950s, things in the tractor-pulling sport got more sophisticated, though the ethos was still "pull on Sunday, plow on Monday" with the same tractor. However, as time went by, those who wanted to win had to modify. Diesel engines were fitted with single turbochargers, then twin turbos, then four; high-horsepower petrol V8s were squeezed into standard tractors, in what would eventually become the Modified class. The Crossbox allowed the installation of multiple engines, and pulling tractors soon appeared with a couple of V8s, then four, then six, then eight!

Present-Day Tractor Pulling
From 1971, American pullers began using the Allison 1708 cubic inches (28 L) V12 aircraft engine, and giant gas turbines weren't far behind—in 1974 the World Speed Record holder appeared on the pulling track with a turbine-engine-powered tractor. Of course, many of these machines were completely unrecognizable as farm tractors, but the standard classes (and later the classic and antique, as well) were kept on in order to keep the sport accessible. Today, a whole host of classes enables all sorts of tractors to take part. So if you like black smoke and lots of noise, go and watch.

How Fast Can A Tractor Plow?

Horse-drawn plow
(medium to heavy soils)
1 acre (0.4 hectare)/day
❖
Horse-drawn plow
(light to medium soils)
1.5 acres (0.6 hectare)/day
❖
Modern 120 hp tractor
30 acres (12 hectares)/day
❖
World plowing record (2005)
793 acres (320 hectares)/24 hours (Case IH Steiger STXQuadtrac, 500 hp)

Slower than a 500 hp tractor, but who's counting?

TRACTOR STATES

Some states used far more tractors than others. In April 1930 the top three were Illinois (69,628 tractors on farms), Kansas (66,275), and Iowa (66,258). The lowest three were New Hampshire (1,096), Rhode Island (589), and Nevada (360).

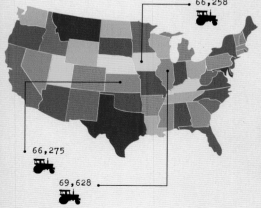

66,258

66,275

69,628

Motor Lift

WHAT DOES THAT MEAN?

Before the Ferguson hydraulic system made it far easier to lift implements, other manufacturers also tried to make the task less back-breaking. Case had its Motor Lift, driven by engine power and allowing one to raise the implement via an enclosed worm gear, operated by a button near the driver's heel. It offered a whole range of implements designed to be used with the Motor Lift, including corn cultivators, beet planters, and mowers.

The kids will never get 'tired' of this!

ALTERNATE USES FOR OLD TRACTOR TIRES AND INNER TUBES

- ★ Playground equipment
- ★ Harbor wall protectors
- ★ Boat hull protectors
- ★ Buoyancy aids (for those who need a really big life preserver)
- ★ Raised flower beds
- ★ Sand pit boundary
- ★ Child's swing

- ★ Retaining wall (filled with earth)
- ★ "Tire sandals"
- ★ Insulation for a garden shed
- ★ Paddling pool for small children. (Drape an old shower curtain over the center and fill with water.)
- ★ Small fountain or pond
- ★ Compost holder

Whatever floats your boat!

Warning! Tractors can give you an inflated opinion of yourself

VIN PLATE

The Vehicle Identification Plate (VIN) is a serial number allocated to each tractor before it leaves the factory, just like the VIN of a car or truck. Since 1981, an international standard for VIN has produced a seventeen-digit number for every vehicle, and tractors are no exception. The VIN plate is usually riveted to the framework of the tractor, somewhere easy to see, and it contains this unique number as well as the engine number and a whole load of other information. Older tractors also have these information plates, but they're often simpler and may be called "manufacturers' plates."

Typical information found on a VIN plate:
- ✪ VIN serial number
- ✪ Engine serial number
- ✪ Date of manufacture
- ✪ Horsepower
- ✪ Rated speed
- ✪ Engine size
- ✪ Gross weight
- ✪ Net weight
- ✪ Patent numbers applicable
- ✪ Factory address

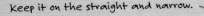

Keep it on the straight and narrow.

Rail Tractor

Tractors that run on rails are used all over the world as railway maintenance vehicles. All "road-rail" vehicles are adapted to be able to run along rail tracks as well as on tarmac. The most common conversion is a set of drop-down steel rail wheels that can be raised and lowered on hydraulics. These are either powered by hydraulic motors or are positioned so that the tractor's own tires are in contact with the rails and do the driving.

Unimogs as well as straight farm tractors are adapted in this way, and they are used for rail-side maintenance in places that are inaccessible by road.

Riding the Rails

It's not just tractors that are used in this way—pickups, trucks, construction cranes, and small utility vehicles are adapted as road-rail vehicles, too. In the United Kingdom, Caseside converted Fordson tractors as shunters, with substantial steel or wooden buffers front and rear to push rows of trucks for short distances. These weren't road-rail vehicles, though—they worked astride one of the rails.

Miles of road to cover? Buy a high-speed tractor.

HIGH-SPEED TRACTORS

A tractor that can cruise the roads at normal traffic speeds was at one time an impossible dream. And, given the state of the average tractor of the 1920s, with steel wheels, no suspension, and sometimes no brakes, one can see why. Even if it were possible to run a tractor on the road at the speed of car traffic, it seemed wasteful to supply tractors with high-speed capabilities (and all the expensive equipment that would make that safe) when they would spend most of their life in the field moving at 5 mph (8 kph).

The weekend starts here—Friday could top 32 mph (51 kph).

Early high speeds

The first glimmerings of a change came with Allis-Chalmers's announcement of a pneumatic rubber tire option on the Model U in 1932. Here was a tractor that could reach a comfortable 15 mph (24 kph) on blacktop without shaking itself, or the operator, to pieces.

On Your Mark. Get Set. Go!

To drive the point home, Allis hired a few celebrity racing drivers, geared up the Model U, and held tractor races at county fairs all over the United States. To the average farmer, who had never seen a tractor travel more than 10 mph (16 kph), the sight of such high-speed machines must have seemed like a thunderbolt from heaven. As if that wasn't enough, in 1933 Ab Jenkins set a new tractor speed record with a Model U—67.877 mph (109.237 kph).

Other manufacturers quickly began to offer pneumatic tires, but no one apart from Minneapolis-Moline really tried to build a truly high-speed tractor. Its 1938 Comfortractor was capable of 40 mph (64 kph) on the road, but it was too expensive to sell in great numbers.

The Trantor is now made by HMT of India.

The Trantor was a result of solid research and fresh thinking.

Post-War Developments

After World War II, the next attempt at a high-speed tractor was the Friday. Launched in 1948, this was built by the Friday Tractor Company of Hartford, Michigan. This three-plow tractor was powered by a 46 hp Chrysler six-cylinder gasoline engine, but its unique selling point was the two-range, ten-speed transmission, which allowed a road speed of 32 mph (51 kph). Alas, like the Minneapolis, it seemed that there wasn't enough demand for a high-speed tractor just then, and the Friday faded away.

Fast-forward twenty-five years. English engineer Stuart Taylor was researching his Masters degree, and discovered that tractors in the United Kingdom spent 50 to 70 percent of their time on transport duties, not in the field. The figures for developing countries were even higher. He reasoned that a new sort of tractor, designed with road haulage in mind, would be far faster and more efficient than a heavier machine primarily designed for plowing at low speed.

The Trantor

The Trantor was the result of this fresh thinking. It was completely different from a conventional tractor, with all-around suspension, truck-style air-assisted brakes, and low weight. Thanks to the fully suspended tow hitch, it could tow a 6-ton (5.4 tonne) trailer at up to 50 mph (80 kph) on the road, but it also had a PTO and could work a two- to three-furrow plow. It was quite unlike the Unimog (a tractor-truck). In 2004, HMT Tractors in India began producing the Trantor, offering 65 to 110 hp.

Fastrac and Moderns

The most successful modern high-speed tractor in the West is the JCB Fastrac, launched in 1991. Better known for its bright-yellow construction machinery, JCB examined the Trantor before coming up with its own take on the high-speed tractor.

The Fastrac was far bigger, heavier, and more powerful than the Trantor, though it shared the concept of all-around suspension, powerful brakes, and had a road speed of 45 mph (72 kph). The coil-spring suspension was self-leveling, to enable the machine to plow a field as well as road haul at high speeds.

Over the years, JCB developed the Fastrac with more transmission choice, more powerful engines, and options like Quadtronic, a four-wheel steering system that improved maneuverability. It remains the most well-known high-speed tractor in the world.

FAST FUTURE?

Today, the true high-speed tractor remains elusive. The Fastrac, despite its success, still only sells in small numbers to a niche market, while Trantor's Indian deal hit political problems. But given a twenty-first century of Peak Oil and global warming, the need for a lightweight, efficient transport tractor like the Trantor is as strong as ever.

Bright yellow success story—Fastrac has sold well for nearly twenty years.

You'll look sweet upon
the seat of a tractor
made for two.

Tandem Tractors

WHAT
DOES THAT
MEAN?

Before four-wheel-drive 100 hp
tractors were commonplace, the
tandem tractor was a shortcut to
producing a high-power all-wheel-
drive machine. It simply consisted
of one tractor hitched to the back
of another, creating a twin-engine
machine, with double the power. The
driver sat on the front or rear
tractor, and controlled both units
from there. In the late 1950s and
early 1960s, tandem hitching became
a popular way for farmers to use
their existing tractors, and
conversion kits were offered to make
the change relatively easy. Ford
offered one that could be used to
convert two tractors into a tandem
in less than ninety minutes, while
in England the Doe company produced
its Triple-D, which was two Fordson
Majors coupled together. Factory
four-wheel-drive tractors spelled
the end of the tandem.

ORANGE GROWERS PIONEERED RUBBER

In the 1920s, orange growers in Florida
found that conventional lugged steel
wheels were damaging the roots of their
trees. So in 1928 they started installing
discarded truck tire casings, usually 8 x
40 inches (20 x 101 cm), over the steels.
Two or three placed side by side
delivered decent traction and flotation.
The idea worked so well that used truck
tires were shipped to Florida in big
numbers for just this reason.

WEIGHT DISTRIBUTION

Front and rear weight distribution is critical for the efficient working of a tractor, and the actual balance varies greatly according to tractor type. This should be split so it is 30 percent front and 70 percent rear on a two-wheel-drive tractor, when one is working from the total ballasted weight (a product of power and travel speed). On a front-wheel assist, the split is 40/60, and, on a four-wheel-drive tractor, the split is 55/45. A weight of 30 percent on the front of a two-wheel-drive tractor doesn't sound like much, but on many machines ballast weight has to be added at the front in order to achieve this.

CAUGHT SPEEDING

Racing driver Barney Oldfield was given a speeding ticket for driving a pneumatic-tired tractor at 10 to 15 mph (16 to 24 kph) through a small town in Indiana in the early 1930s.

Crawlers need balance weights too.

I think, therefore I'm tractor.

WHO COINED THE TERM "TRACTOR"?
The word "tractor" has its origins (as do so many words) in Latin, from the noun trahere, meaning "to pull." The first recorded use of the word with the meaning "an engine or vehicle for pulling wagons or plows," occurred in 1901. On the other hand, some say that Hart-Parr salesman W. H. Williams coined the term "tractor" much later, in 1906, since he felt the term "traction engine" was too long and cumbersome.

MILESTONE TRACTORS

ALLIS-CHALMERS D19

DATES: 1961–1964

WHY IS IT IMPORTANT? IT WAS THE FIRST TURBOCHARGED DIESEL TRACTOR.

ENGINE TYPE: WATER-COOLED, FOUR-CYLINDER, 262 CI (4.3 L)

POWER: 62/67 HP

WEIGHT: 6,835 POUNDS (3,100 KG)

PRICE: $5,834/£3,546 (APPROXIMATELY $42,085/£25,578 TODAY)

GOOD POINTS: GASOLINE POWER WITH DIESEL ECONOMY.

BAD POINTS: IT SOON GOT LEFT BEHIND IN THE POWER RACE.

RANDOM FACT: ONE OPTION (AT $66.95/£40.69, OR APPROXIMATELY $482/£293 TODAY) WAS POWER-ADJUSTABLE "SPINOUT" REAR WHEELS TO QUICKLY ALTER THE REAR TREAD.

HISTORY: If the 1950s saw a power race in the American tractor market (a development that Europe would experience a few years later), then the 1960s saw a full-blown Grand Prix. A horsepower of 45 had once been seen as the power class, but now this was no more than a middleweight. How to meet this insatiable demand for power became a never-ending quest on the part of the manufacturers, and in 1961 Allis-Chalmers tried a new method—turbocharging. Turbos had been around for many years, but no one had tried to turbocharge a production tractor before. Allis needed to bump up the power of its 262 ci (4.3-L) four-cylinder diesel, and a turbo appeared to be the quickest way to do it.

And it was. Power was boosted from 51 hp to 67 hp, almost as much as A-C's 262 gasoline unit. With this power, the turbo, and an eight-speed Power Director transmission, the new D19 Allis caused a sensation when it was launched in 1961. Of course, it wasn't long before a whole string of rival turbo tractors appeared, but A-C was there first.

THIRTY PERCENT MORE POWER—THAT WAS THE SECRET OF
ALLIS-CHALMERS' TURBOCHARGED D19.

Red Tractor Logo

In the United Kingdom, tractors are trusted so implicitly that a Red Tractor logo is used to highlight good food! Assured Food Standards uses the logo on food from farms and companies that meet high standards of food safety and hygiene, animal welfare, and environmental protection. So when British shoppers see the Red Tractor logo on a bag of apples, or a fresh chicken, or a head of broccoli, they know that high standards are guaranteed from farm to package.

"THE JCB SONG"
Artist: Nizlopi
Single: (2005),
a UK No1
What's the Story?
Recalls a childhood
experience of riding
in Dad's JCB. Sold
400,000 copies!

Nebraska tested all the dual-range transmissions.

AMPLI-TORC OR MULTI-POWER?

Dual-range transmissions were the new innovation of the 1950s, and the marketing men had a field day giving them fancy names:

- Multi-Power (Massey-Ferguson)
- Ampli-Torc (Minneapolis-Moline)
- Torque Amplifier (International Harvester)
- Power Director (Allis-Chalmers)
- Triple-Range (Case)
- Hydra-Power (Oliver)

US TRACTOR SALES: HARD TIMES IN THE 1980S AND 1990S

YEAR	TOTAL SALES
1966	185,061
1971	134,070
1972	160,618
1973	196,994
1974	173,801
1975	161,145
1976	153,284
1977	154,893
1978	175,770
1979	188,287
1980	166,078
1981	151,970
1982	119,111
1983	116,933
1984	117,733
1985	115,713
1986	108,795
1987	108,134
1988	106,752
1989	106,575
1990	108,375
1991	93,969
1992	86,852
1993	95,771
1994	106,462

Source: Farm and Equipment Institute

WHAT DOESTHAT MEAN?

Auxiliary Engine

An extra engine—sometimes called a "donkey engine"—was used on early Caterpillar diesel crawlers, and on the John Deere Model R, to help start the main power unit. Electric starting systems of the day weren't powerful enough to start such big diesels from cold, so, on the John Deere, the small donkey engine would be started first to warm up the big engine, until it was ready to fire up. The first John Deere donkey engine was a flat twin, although a V4 was later used. These little engines were designed to run straight up to high speed from cold—quite different from the low-revving twin-cylinder diesel.

Anniversary Specials

Special-edition tractors are sometimes created by manufacturers to mark significant dates. In 1976, to mark the United States' bicentennial celebrations, Case launched a limited edition of the 1570 labeled "Spirit of '76" that was finished in patriotic stars and stripes. Harley-Davidson did the same with one of its motorcycles, and both tractor and bike are now collectors' pieces.

In 2008, CaseIH celebrated fifty years of Steiger with a "Gold Signature Edition" of the big supertractor. Finished in gold, it came as a limited edition with a run of just fifty and wowed the crowds at agricultural shows that year. At the same time, the Case Magnum's twentieth anniversary was marked with a run of one hundred gold-painted special editions. In fact, it was a good year for anniversaries, with Massey-Ferguson also marking its fiftieth.

Just fifty of the Case "Gold Signature Edition" were produced.

"And this month's winner of 'Toss the haybale' is,..."

Chassis Or Not?

The very first tractors had chassis, or frames, on which the engine and transmission were mounted. This was how things were made in those days—cars, trucks, and buses all had chassis as well.

The first tractor to successfully do without a chassis was the Wallis Cub of 1913, whose engine and transmission were mounted on a distinctive U-shape frame of thick boiler-plate steel. It had great strength and rigidity, as well as enclosing the mechanical parts from dirt and water.

Four years later, the Fordson Model F did away with the chassis altogether, using the engine and transmission as a rigid structure to which everything else was bolted. This saved a great deal of weight, although some manufacturers were reluctant to abandon a strong chassis altogether—especially when heavy draft work was involved.

Chassis-less design did become dominant, but beginning in the early 1990s there was a gradual move back toward the chassis. Increasing power outputs was part of the reason, and CaseIH and John Deere reintroduced frames in the 200 to 300 hp range, saying that only a chassis could provide the required strength.

LOADER TOP TIPS

❖ Loaders put a lot of strain on the front axle, especially on two-wheel-drive tractors. On those, increase front tire pressures by 15 psi.

❖ Counterbalance weights, usually cast-iron weights on the linkage, improve stability and reduce steering wear.

❖ A fully laden front loader at maximum height raises the tractor's center of gravity significantly, increasing the risk of overturning. When the tractor is in motion, the loader should be raised high enough for full vision, but not to maximum height.

Power Boost Systems

A power boost system involves use of engine electronics to boost power for PTO (power takeoff) or transport work in certain circumstances. A tractor's ideal power-to-weight ratio (that's the relationship between the all-up weight of the tractor and its maximum power) is around 154 pounds (70 kg)/Kw for heavy field work and about 110 pounds (50 kg)/ Kw for transport and PTO jobs.

Combining these two characteristics in one tractor is the work of the power boost system, which all major tractor manufacturers now offer. CNH's system boosts power at the PTO by 26 hp when the load on the PTO shaft exceeds a certain level. For transport, the extra 26 hp is available in gears thirteen through seventeen, to allow haulage of heavy loads at road speeds. Safeguards prevent the power boost from overloading the tractor; for example, when coolant temperature passes the 225°F (105°C) mark, the system automatically shuts off.

WHAT DOES THAT MEAN?

We can all do with a boost now and again.

International Standards

Tractor testing is now standardized across much of the world, thanks to test procedures laid down by the OECD (Organization for Economic Development). Twenty-nine countries have signed up, including the United States, most of the EU, Iceland, China, Japan, and India. The idea is that any country will accept a tractor test conducted in any other country, making the import and export of tractors much easier.

The OECD tests the following:
- ☆ PTO and engine power
- ☆ Hydraulic power
- ☆ Hydraulic lift
- ☆ Drawbar power and fuel consumption
- ☆ Turning area and turning circle
- ☆ Center of gravity
- ☆ Braking
- ☆ External noise
- ☆ Noise at the driver's position
- ☆ Waterproofing
- ☆ Strength of protective structures (dynamic and static tests)

TOP TIPS
When doing heavy work in the field, gear up and throttle down—use the highest gear that will maintain rated speed.

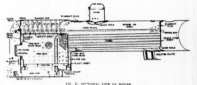

FIG. 1. SECTIONAL VIEW OF BOILER

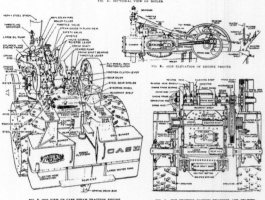

FIG. 2. SIDE ELEVATION OF ENGINE PROPER

FIG. 3. TOP VIEW OF CASE STEAM TRACTION ENGINE

FIG. 4. CUT SHOWING CANNON BEARINGS AND GEARING

COMPLICATED STEAM

Many of the big names in American tractors—such as Case and International Harvester—built steam traction engines long before they moved on to tractors. We like to think of steam as a simple technology, but these were heavy, complex machines. They were expensive, too—only the largest farms could afford to own them, and contractors usually rented them rather than purchasing.

"INTERNATIONAL HARVESTER"
Artist: Craig Morgan
Album: Little Bit of Life (2006)
What's the Story?
A farmer pokes fun at impatient drivers who are stuck behind him on the road.

Sales Talk

A sales leaflet for the Waterloo Boy tractor listed all the claimed advantages over "the old-fashioned, cumbersome and complicated steam traction engine":

1) No possibility of explosion
2) No possible danger of fire
3) No tank man and team necessary
4) A high-priced engineer is unnecessary
5) No early firing to get up steam
6) No leaky flues
7) No boiler repairs of any kind
8) No boiler cleaning
9) No broken bridges on account of weight
10) No waiting for steam
11) No waiting for water
12) No running into holes or other obstructions, because the operator stands in front and has full view of the road before him
13) No time lost making long moves to take on fuel and water
14) No time lost in turning the engine after the separator is uncoupled and left between the stacks
15) No consumption of fuel before starting or after stopping
16) No exact lining with separator necessary
17) No runaway teams on account of "steam blowing off"
18) No long belt to contend with
19) No stopping of the engine when changing from separator to traction.

Mechanical Problems

If anything dogged early tractor owners, it was their machines' reliability (or lack thereof). In 1918 the US Department of Agriculture sent out questionnaires to more than two thousand tractor owners, asking them what gave the most trouble. More than nine hundred answers came back. Magnetos were the worst culprit, with almost one-third of respondents having some sort of "mag" trouble. In fact,

ignition components made up nearly half of the problems, thanks to weak batteries, poor contact points, damp components, and poor insulation.

Magneto	299
Spark plugs	110
Gears	108
Carburetor	104
Bearings	80
Cylinder and pistons	61
Clutch	59
Valves and springs	43
Lubrication	29
Starting	28

Just loping along.

Road Lope

WHAT DOES THAT MEAN?

Road lope is the same pitching or porpoising motion as power hop, but it occurs on the road, not in the field, and has a completely different cause. Road lope is provoked by an off-kilter tire, wheel, or hub, which within a certain narrow speed band will produce a resonance—hence road lope. Because road lope only occurs at certain speeds, it is possible to drive through it by increasing speed until it fades away. Of course, what the operator should do next time is get that wonky wheel fixed.

Grow Your Own Fuel

Tractors can run on fuel that's grown in the same fields that they seed, cultivate, and harvest.

The fuel is biodiesel, consisting of fats or oils that react with an alcohol, usually methanol. The resulting fatty acid, methyl esters, can be distilled to produce a diesel substitute. In Europe, the most common raw material for biodiesel is rapeseed, which yields 343 to 449 gallons (1,300 to 1700 L) of oil per 2.47 acres (1 hectare).

It sounds like the perfect solution to dwindling supplies of fossil fuel—we simply grow the fuel ourselves, making it infinitely renewable. As long as the crops keep growing, this type of oil will never run dry. Biodiesel also produces fewer emissions than oil out of the ground. Production of biodiesel in Germany, France, and Italy has grown rapidly in the past decade, and most tractors will happily run on biodiesel without modification.

Long-Term Sustainable Solution Still Wanted

However, there is a downside. Many point out that crops set aside for fuel cannot be used for food, and that the world is already facing increasing food shortages. To replace all our conventional diesel with biodiesel would entail taking vast areas out of food production. In addition, palm oil gives a higher yield than rapeseed, but the increasing demand for it has resulted in the destruction of tropical rain forest to make way for palm oil crops.

Nothing's ever simple, is it?

Grow your own: in theory tractors can run on fuel from the fields they seed.

FURROW SPANNER

The spanner supplied with the Ferguson Model A was exactly 10 inches (25.4 cm) long, the width of a standard furrow, and was marked out in inches so the operator could use it to measure adjustments in the field.

CYRUS McCORMICK

Most Important Tractor:
INTERNATIONAL FARMALL

The McCormick name isn't quite as recognizable as that of Ford, Ferguson, or Deere, but without Cyrus McCormick there would have been no International Harvester. His father, Robert, had attempted to build an improved reaper, but it was young Cyrus who made it work and patented the result in 1834.

An Opportunity on the Prairies

The McCormick family hailed from Virginia, but Cyrus realized that the really big market for agricultural machinery lay in the Midwest. So he moved to Chicago and in 1847 began making reapers for farmers working the massive prairies. There were setbacks (his brother and business partner died in 1865, and the factory was destroyed by fire a few years later) but the McCormick Harvesting Machine Co prospered. Cyrus died in 1884, but his son carried the business on and in 1902 it merged with Deering Harvester Co to form International Harvester, one of the biggest names in American tractor history.

Four-Wheel Steering

WHAT DOES THAT MEAN?

All four wheels are steerable, with the rear pair steering the opposite way from the fronts. It sounds like a recipe for disaster, but it works! A four-wheel-steer rigid chassis tractor will be able to make tighter turns than a conventional two-wheel steer, and it is an alternative to an articulated setup. Case offered four-wheel steering on its big 4x4 machines in the 1980s, and JCB's Quadtronic system is the only one currently available on a full-suspension tractor. The driver can select one of four modes for Quadtronic:

PROPORTIONAL: The rear axle turns one degree for every two degrees the front axle turns.

TRUE TRACKING: The rear axle steers the same amount as the front axle does.

DELAY: This allows front steering only up to fifteen degrees, for row-crop work.

CRAB: The rear axle steers the same direction as the front, to counteract side slip when traversing hillsides.

A NEW FORD? NO THANKS!
Ford of Britain was kept busy making the Fordson N from 1933, but when they were offered the more up-to-date 9N in 1939 they refused! British farmers loved the old Fordson—about 80 percent of the tractors in Britain were Fordsons by then—and it wasn't until 1952 that it was finally retired.

Belarus tractors used to come from the Soviet Union.

From Russia With Love

Belarus tractors take their name from the now-independent nation in which they're made, which used to be part of the Soviet Union. In USSR days, the badge was used on most Russian-built tractors exported overseas, whether they were wheeled tractors from the Minsk Tractor Works, crawlers from Volgograd, or pivot-steer supertractors from Kharkov.

The Volgograd plant opened up in 1927, at first making a copy of the International 15/30, which the Soviets called the STZ 15/30. Three years earlier, a Russian version of the Fordson F had begun rolling off the lines of another factory in Leningrad. About ten thousand STZ 15/30s per year were made, until the Volgograd plant devoted itself to crawlers beginning in 1937.

Bigger Is Better

The Kirov plant near Leningrad later produced big four-wheel-drive supertractors, and typical was the 7100 that was tested at the University of Nebraska in 1979. Powered by a 1342 cubic inches (22 L) V12 diesel, it mustered nearly 270 hp at the PTO and offered sixteen forward speeds, 1.8 to 21.0 mph (2.8 to 33 kph). They built them big in Russia.

FUEL EFFICIENCY

Average fuel efficiency of tractors (hp-hr/gallon) tested at University of Nebraska

Year	Gasoline/ Distillate	Diesel
1920	5.0	-
1925	5.4	-
1930	5.8	-
1935	6.6	-
1940	9.2	12.5
1950	9.5	13.0
1955	10.0	13.7
1960	9.5	12.3
1965	9.0	12.3
1970	9.5	13.0
1975	8.2	13.0

The Great Ford Conspiracy

The first Ford tractor had nothing to do with Henry. In fact, behind it lay opportunism, bankruptcy, and fraud.

By 1915, Henry Ford's name commanded a lot of respect, yet he still hadn't put his tractor into production. One W. Baer Ewing decided to cash in on this by setting up the "Ford Tractor Company." Of course, it had no connection with the real Ford, but the public didn't know that.

Model "B" for Bankruptcy?

The tractor it produced, the Model B, was not a masterpiece of engineering, and the company soon went into receivership. Undeterred, Ewing tried again, setting up another "Ford" company while his first was still in the bankruptcy courts. Few tractors were made, and the second company soon followed the first into bankruptcy. Ewing's partner, Robert P. Matches, was convicted of conspiracy to defraud investors. And Ewing? At last word, he was in Canada, attempting to set up yet another tractor company.

Ford by name, fraud by nature?

TOP TIPS

When climbing very steep slopes, reverse up if possible—the tractor will not tip over forwards.

4 star, unleaded, or diesel?

METHANE: A FARM-FRESH FUEL SOURCE

Methane gas is an attractive fuel for tractors, because it's renewable and can actually be produced on the farm from the breakdown of organic material such as manure or vegetable waste.

Extracting the methane from this process is relatively simple, using a sealed container or digester that excludes oxygen and allows the gas to be drawn off. It works best at a temperature of 89.6°F (32°C), and digesters are increasingly being built on pig and poultry farms to take advantage of the regular supply of manure.

Like many tractor innovations, farm-produced methane isn't a new idea. Back in 1951, a mixed 220-acre (89 hectare) farm in Germany used manure from cattle, pigs, and poultry to produce 1,500,873 cubic feet (42,500 cu m) of gas a year, enough to not only run two 28 hp tractors but heat the farmhouse as well.

STEIGER
(specs for 1971 Bearcat)

DATES: FROM 1963

WHY IS IT IMPORTANT? THIS WAS THE MOST SUCCESSFUL SUPERTRACTOR.

ENGINE TYPE: WATER-COOLED V8, 636 CI (10.4 L)

POWER: 158 HP

WEIGHT: 19,564 POUNDS (8,874 KG)

PRICE: $48,000/£29,185 IN 1977 (APPROXIMATELY $170,845/£103,881 TODAY)

GOOD POINTS: IT OFFERED PRODIGIOUS POWER AND WORK RATES.

BAD POINTS: ONLY THE BIG FARMS COULD AFFORD ONE.

RANDOM FACT: THE STEIGER BROTHERS LIKED TO NAME THEIR TRACTORS AFTER BIG CATS—TIGER, PANTHER, AND PUMA WERE OTHERS.

HISTORY: The Steiger brothers may not have invented the four-wheel-drive articulated tractor, but they might as well have. In the late 1950s, they were farming 4,000 acres (1,600 hectares) in Minnesota, and they were frustrated that no tractor on the market had enough power to meet their needs. So they rolled up their sleeves and built their own.

They brought together a 238 hp diesel engine with some industrial truck parts and named the result Steiger No. 1. It was a little crude, with tiller steering, but it offered three times the power of any of the mainstream tractors. Soon, the Steigers' friends and neighbors began clamoring for replicas.

What started out as a sideline rapidly turned into a full-fledged business, as Maurice and Douglas Steiger introduced a whole string of four-wheel-drive tractors through the 1960s. All of them included the brothers' own patented power splitter, which allowed the drive train (and therefore the entire tractor) to articulate and give a much tighter turning circle than a rigid chassis would have allowed.

Steiger tractor power and sophistication grew by the year. The biggest Steiger ever tested in Nebraska was the 1978 Tiger III: a 1,150 ci (18.8 L) Cummins, 357 hp at the drawbar, and a thirst for 25 gallons (94 L) per hour under load.

THE STEIGERS BUILT A NEW BREED OF
HIGH-HORSEPOWER SUPERTRACTOR.

Above: Full safety cab didn't help this tractor much. Right: The University of Nebraska led the way in safety cab development.

Safety Cabs

Tractor safety was taken increasingly seriously after World War II, with better brakes and the three-point hitch playing their part. But the biggest step forward was undoubtedly the safety cab. Early cabs did no more than keep the driver warm (once they came with heaters) and dry, but they provided little protection in the event of the tractor toppling over.

Safety cabs, strong enough to withstand a rollover impact, were pioneered by Zetor of Czechoslovakia, which offered them as an option. John Deere was one of the first American manufacturers to provide ROPS (Roll Over Safety Protection).

University of Nebraska Takes the Lead in Promoting Tractor Safety

The University of Nebraska Tractor Testing Laboratory once held an annual Safety Day, showing farmers the effects of rollover accidents. In times past, the effect of a rollover on a cabless tractor was shown by simulating an accident, with a long-suffering dummy named "Jughead" in the driver's seat. And to graphically demonstrate the strength of a modern safety cab, a substantial lump of concrete was swung in by a chain to hit the safety cell. As shown in these demonstrations, safety cabs have saved hundreds, if not thousands, of lives.

"THE TRACTOR SONG"
Artist: Robbie Price
What's the Story?
A familiar one to impatient car drivers all over the world— Robbie curses the tractor he's stuck behind.

It shrunk in the wash!

Small Crawlers

In Britain, there wasn't much demand for bigger crawlers, but the market garden industry (small-scale vegetable growers) used much smaller machines that wouldn't damage delicate crops or create ruts. "MG" means sports car to many people, but it was also the name of Ransomes's range of small crawlers with a little 6 hp single-cylinder engine, which they began building in 1936. ("MG" stood for "market garden.")

In addition to the market garden industry, the small crawler also found a home in Holland. Why? Because it was light enough to be ferried across the drainage dykes in a small boat!

NIGHT WORKING

In the old days, work had to stop when dusk fell. Now, with high-powered spotlights on tractors and combines, it can carry on well into the night. For some jobs, there's no substitute for real daylight, but for farmers under pressure to get the harvest done before the rain sweeps in, working at night can mean the difference between a successful crop and failure.

Is this what's meant by moonlighting?

A Tale Of Three Factories

The Fordson F was made in not one but three factories, though not at the same time.

Fordson built Model Fs in Ireland, but not for long.

Dearborn, Michigan

Henry's Dearborn factory was the first, from 1917, and it churned out seven hundred and fifty thousand of the things.

Fast-forward eleven years. Ford wants to clear the decks to make room for his long-awaited replacement for the Model T. He also wants to set up a plant in Ireland. (Henry was descended from Irish stock, knew that the old country had fallen on hard times, and saw a way of creating a few jobs.)

Cork, Ireland

So Model F production was transferred to a new factory in Cork, and production restarted in 1929. At first, the factory worked at full speed to catch up with a backlog of orders—and the fact that the outdated Model F had been updated as the Model N didn't do any harm either. Alas, sales soon dropped off as the Depression bit. Cork wasn't a cheap place to make a tractor, as most raw materials had to be imported.

Dagenham, England

So in 1933 the Fordson moved again, this time to Ford's rapidly growing site in Dagenham, England. And there it stayed until production of the updated E27N finally ended in 1952.

STEAM FADES AWAY

Steam engine production fell rapidly when tractors came in.

J. I. Case annual production, steam engines (portable and traction)

Year	Number produced
1882	506
1892	572
1902	1,574
1912	2,252
1922	153

Deutz of Germany were diesel pioneers, with a 14 hp diesel tractor back in 1927. For years, they stayed faithful to air-cooled oil-burners, including on this late 1960s D3006.

Takeovers and Mergers

Leaving aside the tractor production giants of the former Soviet Union, China, and India, all the major brands of Europe and North America are in the hands of just five companies, the result of a complex web of takeovers and mergers. The exception is John Deere, the only major name to keep its independence.

AGCO
❖ Deutz-Allis
❖ White
❖ Massey-Ferguson
❖ Fendt
❖ AgChem
❖ Challenger (from Caterpillar)
❖ Valtra

ARGO
❖ Landini
❖ McCormick
❖ Universal
❖ Valpadana

CNH GLOBAL
❖ Fiat
❖ Ford
❖ New Holland
❖ Steyr
❖ Case
❖ International Harvester

SAME-DEUTZ-FAHR
❖ SAME
❖ Deutz-Fahr
❖ Hurlimann
❖ Lamborghini

Half-Tracks

Half-track conversions of tractors—in which standard front wheels do the steering, and short crawler tracks at the back provide traction—enjoyed a brief vogue in the 1950s, before the tractor manufacturers introduced their own four-wheel-drive machines. In England, County and Roadless were two leading conversions, best known for their four-wheel-drive and full-track conversions of Ford and Fordson tractors. These were used for everything from straightforward farm jobs to forestry work and even crossing the high seas!

The simplest conversion used an idler wheel at each side, to turn a Fordson Power Major into a short,

Am I a tractor or a crawler? Just can't decide!

compact six-wheeler. A flexible track was then fitted over this idler and the standard rear tire. This gave far better traction than the standard wheeled setup. The disadvantage of simple half-track conversions was

that they were difficult to steer. Full tracks steer by braking the inside track, but simple half-tracks relied on the standard front wheels.

PULLING A DOUBLE SHIFT

Systems tractors from Fendt and Mercedes were some of the first to offer two jobs in one pass. Today, conventional tractors can provide this service. By attaching two three-point linkages to the tractor—one front, one rear—you can make any machine do two jobs at once, saving time, money, and fuel.

WHAT DOES THAT MEAN?

Intercooler

The intercooler is used in conjunction with a turbocharger, to cool the engine's intake air. Cooler air is denser, so it can be mixed with more fuel to produce more power. Turbos compress air, which heats it up; research done at the University of Nebraska revealed that every 10-degree rise in air temperature reduced power by 1 to 2 percent. An intercooler, using either air or the tractor's own engine coolant to reduce the temperature, circumvents this problem. John Deere pioneered the use of intercoolers on tractors in 1971, and the 4620 increased power from 117 hp at the PTO (for a plain turbo system) to 136 hp.

THE GARDEN TRACTOR EXPLOSION

From the late 1950s a completely new market opened up in the United States, for the garden tractor. A sociologist could tell you why. Suburbia was rapidly growing, as were suburban homes, lived in by affluent folk who didn't want to put in the effort of using a walk-behind mower to cut their expanses of grass. A garden tractor quickly became a status symbol, like the cache of having two cars in the drive instead of one.

The executives at International Harvester were excited by the prospect of selling tractors to all these wealthy suburbanites, and they realized that the market didn't end there. A simple sub-10 hp tractor would also appeal to

Mid-1960s icons—The Beatles, the Ford Mustang, and early garden tractors.

keepers of golf courses, estates, and parks, and even farmers might buy one for mowing and clearing snow around the farm.

They were right—in fact, International Harvester underestimated demand. They reckoned on selling five thousand of the new Cub Cadet

in 1961, but the actual number they sold that year was twenty thousand, and by the end of 1963 over sixty-five thousand had left the factory.

A whole new meaning to mowing the lawn!

GLOBAL SATELLITE POSITIONING

This technology tells car drivers where they are and which turns to take. It guides walkers and mountain bikers—and tractor drivers. But with modern tractors, GPS isn't about finding the right road or track; it's more about maximizing yields. GPS can pinpoint the exact position of a machine in the field to within a meter, and with a combine harvester linked to the yield-recording equipment this can allow the farmer to build up a map of the field, showing up any low-yield areas.

GPS can pinpoint the exact position of a machine in the field to within a meter.

A Tool for More Efficient Farming

Having this information allows the farmer to remedy the problem, whether it be due to poor drainage, or compacted soil, or any number of reasons. On a tractor, these yield maps can be used with the tractor's own GPS to adjust fertilizer or seed distribution according to the yield variation. Data on weed infestation can be used to guide crop sprayers, all with a high degree of accuracy. And that's why they call this "precision farming."

Advanced autopilot systems track front wheel direction and speed.

ON AUTOPILOT

Modern tractors have taken many tasks out of the driver's hands, including gear changing, throttle control, and fertilizer spreading. But what about steering? Yes, that too can be guided by computer. Even the best, most experienced driver will have the occasional lapse in concentration and eventually get tired. The benefit of computer-directed steering is that it allows extremely accurate control despite such lapses.

Computer-directed steering allows extremely accurate control.

GPS Is Your Copilot

The key to all of this is Global Positioning System (GPS), which allows the tractor's position on the ground to be pinpointed with incredible accuracy. And it is incredible—a satellite 12,000 miles (19,312 km) above the surface of the Earth can locate a GPS-equipped tractor to within less than a yard. Even this isn't quite accurate enough for automatic steering, so land-based reference stations are used to refine the position. From up to 6 miles (9.6 km) away, the stations can radio the tractor's exact position to within a few inches.

By 2004, the most advanced autopilot systems on tractors had sensors that track front wheel direction and speed and can even correct for working on a slope. Put together, this information defines the tractor's true route, which is compared to the selected route and any changes in direction made to correct it. This is done by sending a signal to a solenoid valve plumbed into the tractor's hydraulic steering. The result is a guaranteed straight line for plowing, hoeing, or drilling to within 1 inch (2.5 cm).

Such a system cost £30,000 in the United Kingdom ($50,000), but in the UK and United States the cost could soon be recouped for, say, inter-row hoeing—the tractor could work wider and faster, and it was claimed to save time and cut costs by 10 percent. As for the driver, he didn't have to worry—there was still no sign of an autopilot that could take the tractor back to the farm, navigate it along the blacktop or call in at a bar on the way home!

REMOTE CONTROL TRACTORS

A tractor without a driver? In the 1950s, there were several attempts to produce the driverless tractor, and they succeeded—but at the same time the result wasn't much use. Harry Ferguson's engineers enabled a TO-20 to be radio controlled, which was fine, but a man had to stand in the corner of the field doing the controlling, and he might as well have been sitting on the tractor! So why not have one man control two tractors? Surely that would save money, right? Yes, it would, and Ford developed a system that worked. The problem was that controlling one tractor safely and effectively is a skilled job—and controlling two at the same time is well nigh impossible.

Turn Left Ahead

In 1958, a British research team at Reading University seemed to have cracked the problem. They developed an International B250 tractor that could follow a wire buried just below the surface of the ground. This could direct the tractor's steering, and tell it to stop, change speed, or use the power takeoff or the hydraulic linkage. It went into production, but few farmers bought it. They were doubtful about the system's long-term reliability, and there were few situations where tractors had to follow precisely the same lines in the same field, time and again. A couple of orchards did use this guidance system for mower tractors, but that was all.

In the late 1990s, driverless tractors, now with GPS, were back in the news, but there were still some practical barriers to their introduction. Someone still had to drive the tractor into the field and get it going, it was difficult to automate replenishing seed or fertilizer hoppers, and there were safety implications. In the early twenty-first century, the driverless tractor still doesn't have enough advantages to be worthwhile.

PRECISION PROBLEMS

There's just one problem with precision farming—the human factor. GPS systems can deliver huge amounts of data on crop yields, weed distribution, moisture content of the soil, and so on. But all this data isn't much use if it just gets filed away and forgotten. There's an old computer engineer's saying that goes something like this: Data isn't a good thing in itself—it's only useful if it's used!

Put That Data to Work

The same is true of precision farming data. There are so many jobs to do on a farm, that a farmer may not ever have time to delve into data indexing and interpretation. But if the farmer finds a bit of time to store the good data using GPS software that will reproduce it in map form (after

Data from GPS systems is only useful if it's properly anaylzed.

first weeding out any obviously erroneous data, since monitoring systems do go wrong sometimes), he or she can use it to solve problems. Say the map shows a lower-yield area on a field boundary. The farmer can investigate. It could be just rabbits getting through the hedge, in which case the solution is to reinforce the fencing at the boundary, all thanks to data that has been collated, interpreted, and made useful.

Ross or dieselross? They did the same job.

Dieselross

Dieselross means "diesel horse" in German, and does any other phrase more aptly sum up a small, simple workaday tractor? The name was chosen by Hermann Fendt for his first tractor in 1928—really a small single-cylinder stationary engine mounted on a basic chassis. Simple it may have been, but the little Dieselross was reliable and cheap to run, a workhorse that found favor on thousands of German farms.

The company, of course, grew up into Fendt, one of Germany's largest tractor manufacturers, which is now a high-tech arm of the AGCO group. After World War II, Fendt tractors became more sophisticated, but they still carried the Dieselross name.

WHAT DOES THAT MEAN?

Torque Converter

A fluid drive between engine and transmission that can replace a conventional clutch, the torque converter was used by the Case-o-Matic transmission in the late 1950s, to provide up to 100 percent extra pull over direct drive to get through tough spots. The drawback was that it was less efficient than a direct drive. Torque converters didn't get much further in tractors, though Oliver tried the same idea and called it the Lugmatic.

"LIKE A JOHN DEERE"
Artist: Sawyer Brown
Album: This Thing Called Wantin'
and Havin' It All (1995)
What's the Story? Relationships
aren't as straightforward as a
John Deere, as one farm boy
laments.

HITCHING TIPS

❖ Back up squarely to the implement. Don't try to manhandle heavy equipment into position—let the tractor do the work.

❖ Never put yourself between the tractor and implement when hitching. Always work from the side.

❖ The correct hitching sequence on a three-point hitch is left, right, top.

❖ When towing from a swinging drawbar, do not use double jaws on both tractor and implement; this can shear the drawbar pin. Remove half of the jaw from the tractor drawbar.

Sloping Tractor

In 1975, Slope Tractor of Harper, Kansas, began building its Slope Runner, whose axles could tilt up to 30 degrees in either direction, enabling it to traverse slopes without the danger of tipping over.

It came in two sizes. The Slope Runner 1 weighed 5,400 pounds (2,450 kg) and came with an eight-speed transmission offering 1 to 18 mph (1.6 to 29 kph); the Slope Runner 2 was a smaller version, with hydrostatic transmission. Both were powered by Ford four-cylinder industrial engines. Slope Runners weren't farm tractors; they were two-wheel drives with grass tires, intended for mowing motorway embankments and the like.

Gently does it...

How to TRAILER A TRACTOR

in 7 easy steps

Whether it's being hauled to a show, to a new owner, or to the dealer for repair, many tractors have to be strapped onto a trailer. To do this safely so that the tractor can't move around needs some care, but it's quite a simple operation.

1 Drive tractor onto trailer (on strong steel ramps) and park it towards the front, to put some weight on the tow hitch. Parking too close to the front will lighten the steering of the towing vehicle and may even break the hitch. The tractor's parking brake should be on and the tractor left in its lowest gear.

2 Good-quality straps have wear strips to prevent fraying.

3 Mount straps on a solid part of the tractor—tow hitch is the ideal place.

4 Use strap eyes over trailer hooks.

"Growing up on a dairy farm, you certainly learn discipline and a commitment to purpose."

(Mike Johanns, 28th US Secretary of Agriculture)

5 Use strap hooks over trailer lips.

6 Mount straps diagonally, to prevent movement in two directions. Do not finally tighten until all straps are in place.

7 Tie up loose ends.

All tied down and ready to go.

A TINY TRACTOR

Today's lawn or garden tractors aren't new, and back in the 1960s British company Trojan offered the tiny Toraktor. Powered by an American-made Clinton engine of 98cc, the Toraktor wasn't intended for farm use, but really was a serious working tool, rather than a toy—later versions had the sophistication of independent rear brakes and a diff lock.

The little Clinton didn't produce much power, but the Toraktor had just one forward gear topping out at 6 mph (9.6 kph), low enough to pull a substantial load—the Toraktor pictured here once hauled a trailer laden with eighty house bricks, and even towed a Suzuki mini-van out of mud.

There were lots of options for the Toraktor, including its own trailer, and a variety of powered machinery, such as a rotavator. The Clinton didn't have enough guts to do that, so a second engine could be mounted on the back of the tractor. The Toraktor Mk3 cost £127 10 shillings in the UK (£1600/$2550 today), where it was made between 1961 and 1964.

Honey, I Shrunk the Tractor!

HEIGHT = SHORTER

LENGTH = SHORT

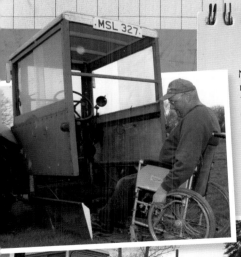

`MSL 327`

A wheelchair tractor

Not many tractors are wheelchair-accessible, and none have been built like that from new. But in 1960, a Mr D. Brunner, who farmed near Henley-on-Thames in southern England, had his Fordson Dexta converted to accept a wheelchair. Mr Brunner was paralyzed from the waist down, having contracted polio as a child, but he also wanted to get around his 400-acre farm.

The tractor's three-point linkage was used to support a lifting platform to support the wheelchair. Mr Brunner would wheel himself in, start the Dexta and raise the platform. All the Dexta's foot controls were converted to hand operation, with linkages extending back to the driver. A total of seven hand levers controlled the platform, gearbox, high/low range, engine start, spool valve, clutch/brakes and throttle. The conversion, carried out by a local company, cost $2400 (£1500), more than the cost of the basic tractor!

Homemade cab is a clue to the nature of this special Dexta.

Tracks pull well in a straight line, but wheels are more adaptable.

TRACKS vs TIRES: let battle commence

Some modern 200 hp+ tractors offer the choice of rubber tracks or conventional pneumatic tires—so which is best? Rubber tracks kick off with a 10–15 percent price premium, which they need to justify, but the short answer to which is best— tracks or tires—depends on a whole list of things: soil type, farm layout, the job in hand, implement type, and so on.

» **Straight-line pull:** A clear victory for the tracked tractor, which in a straight line acts like a wheeled tractor with the diff lock engaged. Tracks reach peak efficency at just 2–5 percent slip, whereas tires require 8–12 percent slip.

» **Turn Under Load:** Here the tables are turned. Wheels perform better under cornering because the 4x4 system ensures that all wheels are transmitting power. On a rubber track system, one track has to slip in order to make the turn.

» **Soil Type:** Tracks perform better on wetter, softer soils, thanks to their ability to gain traction while 'floating' over the top of the soil. But on harder wet soils this floating ability can actually reduce the ability to grip.

» **Compaction:** It is often assumed that rubber tracks are easier on the soil, their larger area resulting in less compaction. But the opposite can be true if they are set up incorrectly, e.g. used with a mounted implement and not ballasted to counter the weight transfer. Especially true when compared to duals.

» **Row Crops:** Tire widths are easier to adjust, and tires tend to mold more easily to furrows.

» **Maintenance:** Tracks need more looking after, though there's no need to set air pressures, and, of course, they never puncture.

» **Field ride:** A win for tracks, whose sheer length means they can span bumps and hollows in the field.

» **Road Ride:** On blacktop, the cossetting ride of soft, air-filled tires is an easy winner. Tracks also transmit more vibration on the road, and wear faster.

» **Maneuverability:** Tracks can turn tighter than tires, but produce more scuff damage in the process.

» **Implements:** Tracks work best with towed, rather than mounted, implements.

» **Summary:** Well, rubber tracks are clearly better than even dual tires under certain conditions, but a properly ballasted wheeled tractor can cope with a wider variety of conditions.

JCB FASTRAC

DATES: FROM 1991 (SPECS FOR 2155)

WHY IS IT IMPORTANT? THIS WAS THE FIRST SUCCESSFUL HIGH-SPEED TRACTOR.

ENGINE TYPE: WATER-COOLED, SIX-CYLINDER DIESEL, 411 CI (6.7 L)

POWER: 137 HP (PTO)

WEIGHT: 15,091 POUNDS (6,845 KG)

PRICE: $106,000/£64,990 (APPROXIMATELY $167,866/£102,102 TODAY) (2009 FASTRAC 2155)

GOOD POINTS: HIGH-SPEED ROAD HAULAGE WITH ACCEPTABLE FIELD WORK.

BAD POINTS: LIMITED MANEUVERABILITY WITHOUT QUADTRONIC.

RANDOM FACT: THE PROTOTYPE FASTRAC USED A TRUCK, NOT A TRACTOR, TRANSMISSION.

HISTORY: A tractor that can haul at normal traffic road speeds was once unthinkable, but now many tractors have a 25 to 30 mph (40 to 48 kph) capability. None of them, however, can touch the Fastrac. Built by JCB, makers of the famous bright yellow digger, it was the first high speed tractor that proved a real success.

Modern farm tractors often spend more time hauling on the road than working in the field, and with ever-bigger farms involving greater distances between fields and stores, a high road-speed capability makes more sense than ever.

JCB wasn't a tractor manufacturer, so it designed the Fastrac from scratch, though it was influenced by the Trantor. The result is like nothing else. Four-wheel drive with full suspension, all-round disc brakes with ABS, and a capability of up to 50 mph (80 kph) made the Fastrac quite unique. The Fastrac's maneuverability was compromised by its rigid chassis, though Quadtronic four-wheel steering helped a great deal. And it wasn't quite as effective in the field as a pure farm tractor. But as a road hauler than can do field work, it has no equal.

FASTRAC REMAINS THE WORLD'S LEADING
HIGH-SPEED TRACTOR.

RAINBOW TRACTORS >>
Traditional colors of the
major makes of tractor.

Fiat: Red/
Black

Ferguson:
Grey

AGCO-Allis:
Orange/Black

TWO JOBS IN A SINGLE PASS

A more versatile take on the conventional machine, systems tractors can have implements mounted at both ends, to allow two jobs to be done at a single pass. The cab is mid- or front-mounted, allowing space for a small load platform at the rear, and drive is by four equal-size wheels.

The idea was first unveiled by Deutz-Fahr and Mercedes-Benz, who both launched systems tractors in 1972. With three-point linkages at both ends, they could carry two implements doing two different jobs at the same time, though this feature later found its way onto conventional tractors as well. The JCB Fastrac was a later systems tractor, with the added benefit of high road speeds.

A tractor that can
multi-task.

TRACTORS IN BOOKS
There are thousands of books about tractors (though none quite like this one). Only a few are not about history, how-to, and technical intricacies. Here are a few of them:

*Love, Sex & Tractors, ROGER L WELSCH

*Everything I Know About Women I Learnt From My Tractor, ROGER L WELSCH

*Women Drive Tractors Too, MARY CARROLL

*Tractors & Chopsticks, ROY S TUCKER

*A Short History of Tractors in Ukranian, MARINA LEWYCKA

| International: Red | Lamborghini: White | Massey Harris:Grey, Green, Red | JI Case: Flambeau Red, White/ Black | Fordson: Grey, Orange, Blue | Allis-Chalmers: Persian Orange |

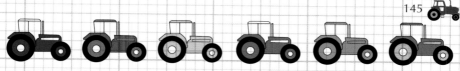

Ford: Blue/ White	Massey-Ferguson Red/ Grey	Minneapolis Moline: Prairie Gold	Oliver: Green/Yellow, Green/White	Steiger: Lime Green	John Deere: Green/Yellow

Twin rear wheels, smooth tires, and high gearing made the industrial Fordson.

INDUSTRIAL TRACTORS

Just as tractors replaced heavy horses on farms, they did exactly the same in factories, docks, and warehouses. It didn't take long to realize that a tractor's hauling ability on a hard surface was better than that of a team of horses, while easier and cheaper to operate than a steam traction engine.

Fordson's industrial version of the Model F was typical, launched in 1923 with solid rubber tires replacing the original steel. The first ones were used as tugs around Ford's factory near Manchester, England. They used a high compression version of the standard Model F four-cylinder engine, running on gasoline only, and to cope with the expected heavy loads, big drum brakes were fitted to the rear wheels. The farm gearing of 4.3 or 7.75 mph (12.47 kph) was too low for road use, so the industrial Fordson had a higher final drive ratio to give up to 25 mph (40 kph). Many of these tractors saw service with the RAF during World War II.

Any color...

Very few manufacturers have ever offered farmers a choice of colors, but a rare exception was Valmet of Sweden. They changed their standard color from red to yellow in 1968, then back to red in 1982. From 1988 the mid-size 505-905 tractors were offered in a choice of five colors: white, blue, yellow, green or red, with black detailing. From 2005 the choice was extended to include four metallics—red, blue, green, and silver.

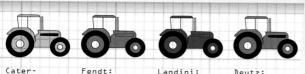

Cater-pillar: Yellow	Fendt: Green	Landini: Blue	Deutz: Green

Four-Wheel Drive Isn't New

From 1916 to 1920, there was a rash of new four-wheel-drive tractors in the United States. But the idea was ahead of its time—these early 4x4s offered far better traction than two-wheel-drive vehicles did, but they were often awkward to maneuver, as the driver had to fight engine torque to steer. So all-wheel drive faded away for forty years, until its destined time.

Early four-wheel drives weren't always all they promised to be.

Some early four-wheel drives:

- » Antigo 1921, 25 hp – known as the "Quadpull," a good name

- » For Drive Fitch, 1916 – just $1,000/£607 (approximately $19,788/£12,016 today), all in

- » Samson Iron Horse, 1919 – soon taken over by GM, not a success

- » Hunter Tractor Co, 1919 – open drive chains were a hazard!

- » IHC – built an experiment six-wheel drive 8-16

- » Kroyer Wizard 4-Pull – steered by clutches each side

- » Lenox Motor Co, 1916 – 30 hp tractor, lasted only two years

- » Morton Tractor Co, 1912 – four-wheel steered tractor-truck

- » Nelson Blower & Furness, 1920 – "self-cleaning" wheels not as described

- » Olmstead Gas Traction, 1912 – awkward tractor, tricky to maneuver

- » Southern Motor Ranger, 1919 – the only four-wheel-drive cultivator

- » Heinze Four-Wheel Drive, 1919 – wheels each side coupled by chain

Fifty years later, 4x4 Unimog (here with Case badges) made a better job of it.

Rated Speed

WHAT DOES THAT MEAN?

Relax, you're at rated speed.

"Rated speed" indicates the engine speed chosen by the manufacturer that is most suitable for the tractor to work at—typically 2200 rpm for a big diesel tractor. The high idle speed (slightly higher than the rated speed) is for running with no load.

Back in 1918, officials decided who got one of these.

SEARS & ROEBUCK'S TRACTOR

America's most famous mail order co., Sears, Roebuck & Company, actually offered a tractor alongside its thousands of other household goods in 1931. It sold the two-plow Bradley GP, which was notable for an early adjustable tread and engine-driven PTO.

GOVERNMENT-ONLY FORDSONS

The Fordson F is renowned as the first tractor that many small farmers could afford. But in its early days it wasn't available to the public and was sold only to governments. The British government had prompted Ford to start making it, in order to boost its wartime food production, and in 1918 Henry announced that the tractor would be sold only to state and national authorities. By May of that year, several US states had made arrangements to allot 7,000 Fordsons. The actual distribution was made through Ford's car dealer network, but the state bureaucracy decided which farmer would get one.

FENDT

"Gt
Die

Torque Rise

WHAT DOES THAT MEAN?

Torque rise measures the difference between a tractor's peak torque and the torque available at rated speed. It's usually expressed as a percentage, using the following formula:

PEAK TORQUE - RATED TORQUE/RATED TORQUE = TORQUE RISE

So a tractor with a peak of 657 pound-feet (298 kg cm), and 425 pound-feet (193 kg cm) at rated engine speed will have a torque rise of 38 percent.

All right, forget the math—the really important thing about torque rise is that it shows how a tractor responds when it hits an extra load (a sticky patch in the field maybe, or a steep hill on the road), and the revs fall off from rated speed. The higher the torque rise, the less the revs will fall and the more responsive and "stronger" the tractor will feel.

THE DIAMOND-WHEELED TRACTOR

The fancy name had nothing to do with gems—it had to do with its wheels. In 1919, the Post tractor company attempted a diamond wheel layout, with two centrally placed driving wheels, one behind the other, and two outrigger support wheels to keep the whole thing upright. A four-cylinder Waukesha engine did the driving, via a chain and bevel gear drive.

Good torque rise will make your tractor feel stronger.

FOUR OR SIX?

LET THE BATTLE COMMENCE

In the 100 hp class, farmers often have the choice of a large six-cylinder nonturbo or a smaller four-cylinder turbo engine, both of which give around the same power. So which is best? A New Holland 457 cubic inches (7.5 L) six and Deutz-Fahr 195 cubic inches (3.2 L) four give the comparison.

BIG SIX PLUS POINTS

This has a smooth, higher torque at low revs, is heavier for better front-end weight distribution, and has a less-stressed power unit.

SMALL FOUR TURBO PLUS POINTS

This uses less fuel for a given output, its more compact engine allows better maneuverability, and it is cheaper to buy.

Six makes sense.

Turbo four is less thirsty.

SPEC COMPARISON

	BIG SIX	SMALL FOUR TURBO
Capacity	457 ci (7.5 L)	195 ci (3.2 L)
Bore x stroke	4.4 x 5 inches (112 x 127 mm)	3.7 x 4.5 inches (94 x 115 mm)
Cylinders	Six	Four
Fueling	Naturally aspirated	Turbo
Power	100 hp	95 hp
Torque	432 Nm	384 Nm
Engine weight	992 pounds (450 kg)	606 pounds (275 kg)

Sixty-six acres an hour—
that's two month's work for a
horse-drawn plow.

WORLD CULTIVATION RECORD

Records are made to be broken, but as we went
to press, the world record for the most land
cultivated in twenty-four hours stood at 1,591
acres (644 hectares). It was set in 2007 by an
AGCO Challenger MT875B hauling a set of
Gregoire Besson XXL discs, 46 feet (14 m) wide—
they covered 286 miles (460 km), or enough
ground to cut a strip, 6 inches (15.2 cm) wide,
around the equator.

Put another way, the area was equivalent to
780 soccer fields, or 66 acres (26.8 hectares) per
hour. Fuel consumption was 1.16 gallons (4.42 L)
per hectare.

Power Shift

WHAT DOES THAT MEAN?

Also known as "shift-
on-the-go," power
shift allows
clutchless gear
changing while on the
move. Transmissions
may be partial power
shift, with clutchless
changes between
ranges—typical is a
sixteen-speed setup
with power shift
across four ranges.
Full power shift
offers shift-on-the-
go between every ratio
in the box. Power
shift first appeared
in the 1950s, when
tractors began to
offer twin ranges
with shift-on-the-go
between the two.

TRACTOR SEATS

Early tractor seats were no more than steel pans, designed for economy rather than comfort. In fact, it was considered less than manly to add a cushion—and some drivers even opted to stand all day rather than sit.

Gradually, though, tractor makers did start to consider comfort, and in the early 1950s they began to introduce shock absorbers, coil springs, and padding to make those long hours at the wheel a little more comfortable. One interesting variation was the swing seat offered by Minneapolis-Moline—it could be swung out of the way, giving the driver the option of standing for better visibility.

Yesterday's Discomfort, Today's Collectible
Today, modern tractor seats are comfy enough for working all day, but those old steel pans, cursed by generations of drivers, have become highly collectible.

Some traders sell nothing else but old tractor seats, and there's a thriving business in brand-new replicas.

Best seat in the house?

What's underneath the CAB?

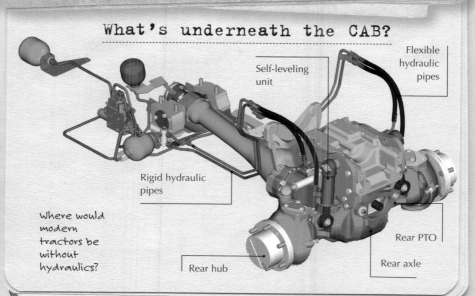

Self-leveling unit

Flexible hydraulic pipes

Rigid hydraulic pipes

Where would modern tractors be without hydraulics?

Rear hub

Rear PTO

Rear axle

Ready to plow at 45,000 rpm, the turbine-powered Ford Typhoon.

Turbine Tractors

The idea of a gas turbine tractor gained brief popularity in the late 1950s and early 1960s, but it never got beyond the prototype stage. It was a beguiling, futuristic idea at the dawn of the modern era, but it was ultimately doomed to failure.

The advantages of a gas turbine over a conventional piston engine include an uncanny smoothness, good acceleration, high power, compact size, and low weight. And a turbine can also run on a variety of cheaper fuels such as paraffin.

Few of these advantages have much relevance to tractors, though. Tractors don't need to accelerate fast, ultimate smoothness isn't a big issue, and a bulky, heavy engine can be a boon. In addition, gas turbines are more expensive to build than diesel. And, even if they could run on a cheaper fuel, they used more of it.

Prototypes in Abundance—Some Successful, Some Not
Undeterred, both Ford and International unveiled gas turbine prototypes. Ford's Typhoon used a free-piston turbine that whizzed around at 45,000 rpm and was de-rated to half its original 100 hp. Long forgotten at the back of a Ford warehouse, the prototype ended its days in a recycling bin.

International's stab at a turbine tractor was the HT-340, which certainly looked the part, with its sloping nose bonnet. The prototype attracted massive publicity for International. In all the excitement about the turbine, many people overlooked the HT-340's equally revolutionary hydrostatic transmission, which worked well and was used on International production tractors for many years.

CATERPILLAR CHALLENGER

DATES: From 1986 (specs for Challenger 65)

WHY IS IT IMPORTANT? It was the first tractor with flexible rubber tracks.

ENGINE TYPE: Water-cooled, six-cylinder diesel, 638 ci (10.5 l)

POWER: 270 hp (PTO)

WEIGHT: 31,000 pounds (13,950 kg)

PRICE: $140,000/£85,119 (approximately $275,520/£167,506 today)

GOOD POINTS: Crawler traction with reasonable road speeds.

BAD POINTS: Traction is not always better and needs careful setting up.

RANDOM FACT: Rubber tracks are solid, so there is no air pressure or punctures to worry about.

HISTORY: For years, Caterpillar did quite a good job of persuading a few farmers to buy a crawler instead of a wheeled tractor. Where conditions were really slippery, these machines performed better. But the traditional metal-tracked crawler had miserable performance on the road, and the tracks wore out quickly. Meanwhile, the advent of four-wheel-drive tractors saw farmers abandon metal tracks for good.

Caterpillar thought it had the answer, with the Challenger. Launched in 1986, this used rubber tracks reinforced with steel cables.

The system was called Mobil-trac, and Caterpillar claimed that it offered the best of both worlds—crawler traction in the field and near-wheeled performance on the road.

Despite considerable skepticism at the time (farmers are a skeptical breed), the Challenger proved itself, and Cat expanded the line, while rival tractor manufacturers followed up with their own rubber track conversions of existing tractors.

The Mobil-trac system might not have lived up to all of its claims, but it was a real milestone and has stood the test of time.

CATERPILLAR KICKED OFF THE RUBBER TRACK REVOLUTION
WITH THE CHALLENGER.

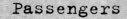

Passengers

Traditionally, tractors have been one-person vehicles. If a passenger wanted to go along, he or she would have to stand on the platform, or perch precariously on one of the rear wings. Things were different in France and Germany in the 1950s, where tractors invariably provided a flat top and hand holds on each wing, so that the operator could take a couple of people along for the ride. (Most likely, some tractors were still being used as transportation to town on market days.)

Modern tractors often have a token passenger seat in the cab that usually folds up out of the way. In 2001, *Profi* magazine surveyed what was available, make by make:

❖ **Case CS:** Rubber-covered fold-up seat of ample size

❖ **Deutz/SAME:** Built-in backrest

❖ **Fendt:** Clever folding, standard seat belt, but not comfortable

❖ **John Deere:** Seat suspended, but poor folding

❖ **New Holland:** Quick-fold, basic plastic seat

❖ **Massey-Ferguson:** Proper padded seat

Count 'em—three on the tractor, four on the trailer.

Diff Lock

A diff lock, as the name suggests, locks the differential, so that both wheels on the same axle rotate at the same speed. A diff's job on any vehicle is to allow wheels to rotate at different speeds, so that they can turn corners without tire scrub. That's all very well, but in slippery conditions this allows the wheel with least grip simply to spin. To prevent this, the driver turns the diff lock on, so that power is fed to both wheels equally. Diff locks are often automatic on modern tractors, with sensors detecting excessive wheel slip and switching the diff lock on or off as needed.

"JOHN DOE ON A JOHN DEERE"
Artist: Lonestar
Album: Crazy Nights (1997)
What's the Story?
In this variation on a familiar theme, a farm girl in the city realizes she's pining for a country boy back on the farm.

TOP TIPS

When reversing a trailer, initially steer in the opposite way you want the trailer to turn. Sounds crazy, but it works.

HIT AND MISS

It was not used on tractors, but the hit-and-miss governor was a familiar sight on farms in the early twentieth century. It controlled the running of small, crude stationary engines that were used to run wood saws, water pumps for irrigation, or generators. A hit-and-miss governor kept the engine at a set speed by holding the exhaust valve open whenever the engine ran too fast. As it slowed down, the valve was closed again, allowing the engine to fire—hence, the term "hit and miss."

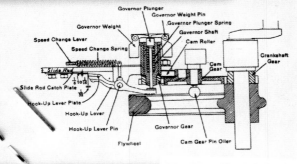

PLOWS: THE OLDEST TOOL

The plow is one of the oldest tools known to mankind, and it has been an instrument of agriculture for most of recorded history. Its job is to turn over the upper layer of soil. This process aerates the soil and allows it to hold moisture better; weeds and the remains of previous crops are buried, allowing them to break down. New soil is exposed, and fresh nutrients are brought to the surface.

As long as farmers grow food, they have to plow.

New Developments: Reversible Plow, and the Three-Point Hitch

Early single-direction plows could turn the soil on the right only, but they were later superseded by the reversible plow, with an extra (left-handed) set of mold boards, which is still the basis of the modern tractor plow. When one side is working, the other is carried upside down. At the headland, as the tractor turns, the plow is raised and turned over, so that the field is worked in a continuous path.

Before the three-point hitch came along, plow depth had to be adjusted manually with screw handles. It wasn't until the mid-1950s that Harry Ferguson's patents finally ran out, and other plow and tractor makers were able to adopt his hydraulic three-point hitch, with automatic depth control for plowing.

The AGCO Phenomenon

Most tractor brands are long established and long lived—names like John Deere, New Holland, Massey-Ferguson, and Deutz can trace their ancestry back for decades, and in some cases well over a century.

AGCO is different—twenty years ago, it didn't exist. It started off as a management buyout of Deutz-Allis, the US arm of Deutz-Fahr. AGCO grew rapidly, not just by increasing its sales, but by buying up existing tractor makers. It bought White in 1991, as well as Fiat's Hesston operation. Three years later, it doubled its size overnight by acquiring Massey-Ferguson, and in 1997 it reinforced its European arm by swallowing up Fendt, and then AgChem in 2001. Other acquisitions of combine, implement, and sprayer manufacturers have given AGCO a complete lineup of farm machinery.

It hasn't all been plain sailing—AGCO has closed factories as well as bought them—but its rapid rise from management buyout to one of the biggest tractor makers on the planet is an impressive one.

AGCO rose from minor league buyout to world player in twenty years.

Early Accidents

Early tractors were often accidents waiting to happen. The Rumeley Oil Pull for example, had an open platform on which the operator stood, with nothing to stop him from stumbling backward, straight into the path of the towed implement.

But the most common accident involved rolling over or tipping backward. The former could happen when a tractor was traversing steep slopes. The latter could happen when the towed implement hit an obstruction—the implement would come to a dead stop while the tractor reared up, and if the operator didn't declutch quickly enough the tractor could tip right over backward, often with fatal consequences.

Rumeley Oil Pull's open platform could be lethal if the driver stumbled backward.

WHAT DOES THAT MEAN?

Four-Wheel Drive

Four-wheel drive—in which all wheels are driven by engine power—is fundamental to the modern tractor, and, apart from lawn tractors and other low-power machines, most tractors now use it. It's all a question of grip. A tractor feeling its way through a wet field, or hauling a heavy trailer up a muddy track, needs all the grip it can get. If all four wheels are driven, instead of just two, this doubles the chances of at least one wheel finding traction. This function is just like that of four-wheel drive on the average road-bound SUV, although in this case it is doing a useful job!

REAL HORSEPOWER

The term "horsepower" was coined by James Watt, as a device to help market his improved steam engine. Back in the eighteenth century, everyone was familiar with the power of a single horse, so he calculated the work that a typical horse could do and described his engine in terms of how many horses it would replace.

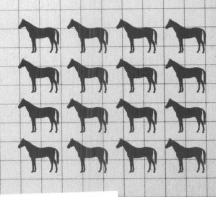

The Cub is obviously more interesting than its big brother.

WATER BALLAST

❖ This is a cheaper alternative to cast-iron weights, although it is a more laborious process. Using a special adapter for the tire valve, it's possible to partly fill the tires with water, to increase ground pressure and traction.

❖ Tires are usually filled to the three-quarter mark (up to the valve when the valve is at its highest point) and calcium chloride or another antifreeze element is added to protect the water from frosting. The remaining air in the tire is inflated to normal pressure, but it should be checked more regularly than normal.

❖ A 13.6/12-36 tire that is 75 percent liquid ballasted will have 419 pounds (190 kg) of added weight.

LITTLE AND LARGE

By the 1960s, International Harvester was making a huge range of tractors. Like any manufacturer, it couldn't afford to miss out on developing markets like those for garden tractors and giant four-wheel drives, as well as the more conventional farm tractors in between.

	CUB CADET 70	4300 DIESEL
Engine type	Single-cylinder air-cooled	Six-cylinder water-cooled
Power	7 hp	180 hp (drawbar)
Transmission	Single-speed	Eight-speed
Front tires	4.80-8	23.1-26
Rear tires	6-12	23.1-26

SQUARE TURN'S SECRET

The Square Turn tractor, built in the early twentieth century, could do tight hairpin turns at the end of the field. It did this despite its massive front driving wheels and a reasonably long wheelbase. The Square Turn's secret was a system of fiber-faced driving cones that enabled one drive wheel to turn forward while the other turned backward.

So, like a crawler, the Square Turn could spin around in its own length. Not that this capacity helped the company survive—in 1925, the assets of the Square Turn Tractor Company were sold off at a sheriff's sale for a mere $15,000/£9,106 (approximately $184,000 /£111,731 today).

The Square Turn tractor could turn around in its own length.

TOP TIPS

On the road, if the traffic's backed up behind your tractor, stop and let them past—they'll all think better of tractor drivers if you do.

"JOHN DEERE TRACTOR"
Artist: The Judds
Album: Give A Little Love (1987)
Greatest Hits, Volume 2 (2004)
What's the Story?
A farm girl moves to the city with high hopes, but urban life isn't what she expected.

Make sure you get the right one.

THREE-POINT HITCH CATEGORIES

There are five different hitch sizes, called categories. The higher category hitches have sturdier lift arms and larger connector pins. There is some overlap in the tractor horsepower from one category hitch to the next.

CATEGORY	TRACTOR HP	TOP LINK PIN DIAMETER	LIFT ARM PIN DIAMETER
0	Up to 20	5/8 inch (1.58 cm)	5/8 inch (1.58 cm)
1	20 to 45-55	3/4 inch (1.9 cm)	7/8 inch (2.2 cm)
2	45-55 to 90-95	1 inch (2.54 cm)	1 1/8 inches (2.86 cm)
3	90-95 and up	1 1/4 inches (3.17 cm)	1 7/16 inches (3.65 cm)
4	180-400	1 3/4 inches (4.37 cm)	2 inches (5 cm)

 WHAT DOES THAT MEAN?

Power Hop

With power hop, also known as "wheel hop," "tire hop," or "tractor hop," the tractor pitches fore and aft increasingly violently when under heavy draft load in the field. It's a scary phenomenon for the driver, who will usually throttle off before the hops become severe enough for a loss of control. Power hop only came to light when big four-wheel-drive tractors were introduced in the US in the late 1950s; two-wheel-drive machines are not affected by this phenomenon. The cure for power hop depends on many variables, including tire pressures, soil condition, and whether the tractor has front suspension.

TOP TIPS
Good tractor drivers never need to apply the brakes fiercely.

PNEUMATICS VS. STEEL VS. SOLID RUBBER

It was an easy victory for low-pressure pneumatic rubber tires, though it took several years before they became the universal tire of choice for tractors.

Why were they so much better than all of the alternatives? Because low-pressure pneumatics offered the best of both worlds: comfort and speed on the road, plus good traction and high efficiency in the field. An Allis-Chalmers WC was found to be 25 percent more fuel-efficient on rubber than on steel and could operate in third gear instead of second with the same load.

Early experiments used high-pressure truck or aircraft tires, which gave good on-road performance but little grip in the field. Only the tractor-specific tire, with low enough pressure to mold itself around lumps and bumps, and big rubber lugs, did the job.

» **Steel:** Good field traction; slow, bumpy, and uncomfortable on the road.

» **Solid rubber:** Terrible field traction and slow on road; best suited for factory tug tractors.

» **High-pressure rubber:** Early experiments with truck tires on tractors delivered good on-road performance, but very poor performance in the field.

» **Low-pressure rubber:** The Holy Grail—fast and comfy on tarmac and good grip in the field.

The winner! Low pressure rubber proved better all round.

HOW MANY CYLINDERS?

❂ One cylinder: Simple, but lacked smoothness and flexibility

❂ Typical Single: Lanz Bulldog

❂ Two-cylinder: Compact, smoother than a single

❂ Typical Twin: John Deere Model B

❂ Three-cylinder: Now popular in compact diesel tractors

❂ Typical Three: Ford 4000

❂ Four-cylinder: The standard unit for sub-100-hp tractors

❂ Typical Four: International 354

❂ Six-cylinder: Standard unit for all tractors with 100 hp and above

❂ Typical Six: John Deere 7610

❂ V8: Very smooth, favored for some two-wheel drives in early 1970s and supertractors in the 1980s; no longer used.

❂ Typical V8: Massey-Ferguson 1150

❂ V16: Heavy, complex, powerful, only used by one tractor

❂ Typical V16: Big Bud 16V-747

Threshing accidents

Threshing machines were dangerous, especially in the early days, when laborers weren't used to fast-moving machinery. Worse still, their drink of choice was beer, and six pints might be consumed in a day. Contemporary reports tell of intoxicated workers getting caught up in the machinery and losing the shirt off their backs, or much worse. A January 21, 1846, article in the *Bury and Norwich Post* reported the following mishap: "There was a shocking accident at Lodge Farm in Glemsford in occupancy of Mr Morley. A poor woman being employed to work on a threshing machine had her clothing caught in the machinery and one of her legs was drawn in and dreadfully mangled, amputation was resorted to and hopes are entertained about her recovery. She was aged about 68 years."

NOISE CONQUERED

Average in-cab noise of tractors tested by University of Nebraska

Year	Sound levels dB(A)
1970	93.7
1971	89.1
1972	86.3
1973	85.0
1974	84.0
1975	87.2
1976	83.0
1977	80.3
1978	80.9

JEROME CASE
Most Important Tractor: CASE 15-27

Jerome Increase Case was a man of many parts. Mayor of Racine three times, he served as a state senator, founded the Wisconsin Academy of Science, Arts and Letters, and was president of the agricultural societies for both Wisconsin and Racine. In between he was an inventor who built enough threshing machines to become known as the "Threshing Machine King."

A True Do-It-Yourselfer
He was a hands-on man, too. One story has it that in 1884 a local dealer couldn't repair a faulty Case thresher. Case (then sixty-five years old) traveled straight down to sort the problem out and, when unable to cure the fault himself, promptly burned the rogue machine to the ground and ordered a brand-new replacement, which arrived the following day! By the time Mr Case died, his company was the biggest maker of steam engines in the world—it would go on to be a leading tractor manufacturer as well.

PRODUCTIVITY PROGRESS

Work hours to produce 1.1 tons (1 tonne) wheat, and yields: 1885-1999

YEAR	WORK HOURS	TONS PER 2.47 ACRES (TONNES PER HECTARE)
1885	90	2.0 (2.2)
1900	38	1.9 (2.09)
1925	30	2.5 (2.75)
1945	20	2.6 (2.86)
1965	10	4.4 (4.85)
1985	8	6.0 (6.61)
1999	7	7.5 (8.26)

Upgrade Your Transmission

Before International Harvester offered the Farmall MTA, with its two-range, ten-speed transmission, M-W Gear, Inc. produced an upgrade kit to convert the standard five-speed Farmall to a nine-speed. Designed for dealer installation, it added four higher ratios, giving 6, 7.75, 9, and 11 mph (9.6, 12.4, 14.5, and 17 kph), with two reverse speeds, two PTO speeds, and two power lift speeds. "Rigorously field tested under actual working conditions. Gears unconditionally guaranteed for 90 days ... It's money in your pocket," went the M-W Gear marketing language.

Hydrostatic Transmission

WHAT DOESTHAT MEAN?

Hydrostatic transmission drives the wheels, not through gears and driveshafts, but by hydraulics. This is no longer used on big farm tractors but is almost universal on lawn and garden tractors. International Harvester was a pioneer of hydrostatic transmission, with its gas turbine-powered HT-340, and went on to sell a whole range of "Hydro" tractors beginning in 1967. This gave an infinitely variable transmission, with ground speed and forward/reverse controlled by a single lever. It proved ideal for yard work (that required plenty of shuttling back and forth) and for field jobs that demanded a constant speed.

Keep The Cup Full

Before the days of reliable oil pumps and force-feed lubrication, tractors were kept lubricated by oil or grease cups, little reservoirs of lube that supplied the engine either by gravity or by screwing down the top. They often had glass windows, for at-a-glance checking. Later, the Madison-Kipp Lubricator offered automatic pressure lubing of all bearings at an adjustable rate. Hart Parr used this device on its tractors, and a sight glass on the lubricator allowed the tractor driver to check that oil was being delivered. It was a step forward from the oil cups, but the Madison-Kipp was not perfect—once the oil had done its work, it simply dripped onto the ground. However, this was soon replaced by force-feed recirculating oil systems, which saved the black gold and reused it.

Half-full or half-empty?

Weights

Solid steel weights are either bolted onto the front or rear wheels of a tractor or mounted on the front or rear of the machine. When we're all talking about fuel efficiency and the need to reduce vehicle weight, it seems odd to see farmers actually adding weight to their tractors. However, there's a very good reason. A tractor's efficiency depends on good traction, and in difficult conditions this can be improved by adding weight to front or rear axle—hence the removable weights. The operator (if he or she is sufficiently conscientious) will add or remove weight to provide exactly the right amount of ballast for each job. An over-ballasted tractor will feel sluggish; an under-ballasted one will suffer from too much wheel slip.

Tractor Pulling Classes

(Illinois Tractor Pulling Association)

* **Super Stock Garden Tractors** – Single-cylinder/1,050 pounds (477 kg) maximum weight
* **Limited Mini Rods** – Gasoline V8/1,800 pounds (818 kg)
* **Mini Rods** – Supercharged up to 575 ci (9.4 L)/2,000 pounds (909 kg)
* **Antique Tractors** – Pre-1940, 5,500 pounds (2,500 kg)
* **Classic Tractors** – Pre-1953, 5,500 pounds (2,500 kg)

* **Farm Stock Tractors** – Up to 466 ci (7.6 L)/9,500 pounds (4,318 kg)
* **Farm Stock Tractors** – No capacity limit/12,000 pounds (5,455 kg)
* **Super Farm Tractors** – Up to 640 ci (10.4 L)/9,300 pounds (4,227 kg)/24.5-inch (62 cm) rear tire
* **Limited Pro Stock** – Up to 466 ci (7.6 L)/3x4 turbo/8,200 pounds (3,727 kg)
* **Pro Stock** – Up to 680 ci (11.1 L)/diesel only/10,000 pounds (4,545 kg)

* **Super Stock** – Diesel or alcohol/6,000 pounds (2,727 kg)
* **Super Stock** – Diesel or alcohol/8,200 pounds (3,727 kg)
* **Super Stock** – Diesel only/9,700 pounds (4,409 kg)
* **Modified Tractors** – Car or aircraft engines/5,800 pounds (2,636 kg)
* **Modified Tractors** – Car or aircraft engines/6,000 pounds (2,727 kg)

BADGE ENGINEERING

Don't judge a tractor by its badge.

Imagine you're a tractor manufacturer. You have a gap in your lineup of tractor models, but it could take years to design a machine to fill it. What do you do? The quick and obvious answer is to engage in a little "badge engineering": buy a tractor model from an archrival, and sell it as one of your own. It just goes to show that even tractors aren't always what they seem. Here are a few real examples:

Decade	Sold As	True Identity
1950s	Massey-Ferguson 95	Minneapolis-Moline G705
1960s	Oliver 500	David Brown 850
1970s	Allis-Chalmers 160	Renault
1980s	Long (whole range)	UTB of Romania
1990s	Fiat G-series	Ford 70 series

MILESTONE TRACTORS

MASSEY-FERGUSON 3000 SERIES

DATES: FROM 1987 (SPECS FOR 3090)

WHY IS IT IMPORTANT? ITS PIONEERING USE OF ELECTRONICS

ENGINE TYPE: WATER-COOLED, SIX-CYLINDER, 354 CI (5.8 L)

POWER: 95 HP (PTO)

WEIGHT: 10,400 POUNDS (4,717 KG)

PRICE: $41,000/£24,906 (APPROXIMATELY $77,846/£47,342 TODAY)

GOOD POINTS: LOTS OF USEFUL INFORMATION WITH AUTOMATIC CONTROLS.

BAD POINTS: BRINGS WITH IT THE POSSIBILITY OF ADDING MORE ITEMS THAT CAN GO WRONG.

RANDOM FACT: MASSEY-FERGUSON WAS AN ANGLO CANADIAN NAME, BUT THE 3000 WAS MADE AT BEAUVAIS IN FRANCE.

HISTORY: Remember the days before electronics? They did exist, but in 1987 Massey-Ferguson wowed the tractor world with the new 3000 series. What was special about the 3000 was that it made more use of electronics than any previous tractor. In the 1970s, some combines had offered electronic systems monitoring, but the new MF took that concept one step further, with electronic control systems as well.

It was called Datatronic, and it monitored sixteen lines of data, from engine speed to fuel reserve (in hours) to wheel slip and acres worked per hour. This much was just a logical extension of previous electronic packages, but Datatronic's real leap was to use this same information to control the rear linkage and wheel slip.

Wheel slip control was automatic, comparing wheel speed with actual forward speed, then adjusting the plow's working depth or tractor power if the slip was excessive. And it would do the opposite if wheel slip was less than the optimum figure. All the driver had to do was set the parameters before starting work. Some say that electronics are too complex and take the skill out of farming, but the bottom line is that they do a good job.

THE ELECTRONIC CONTROL ERA BEGAN WITH THIS TRACTOR.

Standards are slipping, and so they should be (but not too much).

TOP TIPS

When parking, apply the hand brake, put gear lever in neutral and lower implements and loaders to the ground.

WHAT DOES THAT MEAN?

Wheel Slip

Tractor wheel slip is just what it sounds like—a situation in which the wheels spin on a slippery surface, faster than ground speed. That might sound like a waste of energy, but some wheel slip is actually a good idea.

With no wheel slip at all in tricky conditions (something that's possible with heavy ballasting), the transmission becomes overloaded with torque; the tires will last a lot longer, but the transmission surely won't.

The answer is to ballast so that the wheels slip a little and give the tires some more work to do—it's what they are designed for. The handbook will tell you the recommended wheel slippage for particular conditions, but generally it's in the range of 8 to 12 percent for two-wheel-drive tractors and 10 to 15 percent for four-wheel drives.

An Amphibious Tractor

Hope this is the shallow end!

So, a standard Super-4 was waterproofed with special oil seals, a sealed clutch housing, and modified air cleaner. The electrics were removed and the engine was started by hand using a Simms inertia starter. To prevent the Sea Horse from sinking to the seabed, it was given big flotation tanks front and rear, with extra buoyancy provided by watertight compartments in each wheel.

A tractor that can cross oceans sounds very unlikely, but the County Sea Horse could certainly swim, and it really did cross the English Channel! In the early 1960s, County were best known for their four-wheel-drive tractors based on Fordson skid units. They reasoned that an amphibious version that was equally at home in swamps, bogs, water, sand, or snow would find a ready market.

Would It Really Swim? And Would It Sell?

Initial trials went well (once the Goodyear rice tires had been reversed in order to give good forward motion) and County executives decided to publicize the tractor by having it crossing the Channel in July 1963. With technical director David Tapp at the wheel (or the helm, in this case) it made the crossing in just under eight hours. It was then put to work harrowing a field, just to prove that it was still a working tractor.

It was an impressive feat and attracted a lot of publicity, but very few Sea Horses were actually sold.

Like A Rolling Stone

Stony soil is the enemy of farmers. It's hard on implements, hard on tires, and hard on fuel, especially when it includes sharp flints. One farm in Yorkshire, England, based on flinty, loamy soil, found that standard tractor rear tires lasted for only a thousand hours, or a season's work. When being used for plowing, the tires could only manage 494 acres (400 hectares), and they came to expect three or four punctures every year. A new type of severe service tire from Firestone lasted nearly twice as long, and didn't puncture at all in eighteen months. Still, it just goes to show that, despite all our technology, farmers still have to adapt to nature.

Stones are the farmer's enemy.

NEBRASKA TESTS

Choremaster was Nebraska's smallest ever test machine.

For decades, the University of Nebraska has tested every model of tractor for sale in the US. From the Waterloo Boy in April 1920 to the very latest machines, nothing has escaped the eagle eyes of the testers.

Test track was extensive.

Nebrasaka's Biggest & Smallest

	Choremaster B	Big Bud 525
Date Tested	1950	1981
Engine	5.89 ci	1150 ci
	(96 cc)	(18.7 L)
Power	1.47 hp	421.5 hp
Transmission	1 forward	9 forward
Weight	123 pounds	51,920 pounds

The Cheating Tractor Problem

The University of Nebraska tractor tests came about in the early twentieth century because many farmers were being cheated. Persuasive traveling salesmen would sell them a tractor and then disappear. When the tractor needed a spare part or failed to live up to the salesman's extravagant promises, the company could not be found either.

The trouble was, back in the early years of the twentieth century, tractor manufacturers could claim whatever they wanted, and there was no means of verifying their claims. And early tractors often didn't live up to those promises, because the tractor boom had attracted a whole crowd of ne'er-do-wells whose tractors were heaps of junk. Some "tractor companies" didn't even make anything—they would just sell stock to unsuspecting investors and then disappear with the proceeds.

Winning team of Nebraska's annual "Hunt the Swarf" competition.

Bow ties or trilbies were de rigeur during belt testing.

John Deere Engineers observe the belt test of the John Deere Model R Tractor.

There's always one bit left over!

NEBR. 4-H LEADERS TRAINING MEETING 1949

National Standards

The solution to the problem of false claims about tractors was a set of independent tractor tests, to enable farmers to compare different machines and know that the figures were trustworthy. One man who was inspired to see this job through was Wilmot F. Crozier, who had bought two tractors that were seriously substandard and one that actually delivered more power than it claimed.

He helped push through the Tractor Test Bill in 1919, which stated that any tractor sold in Nebraska had to be tested first, undergoing a standard routine at the State University. The first test scheduled for the fall of 1919 was abandoned due to snow, but they soon got going in the spring. So useful were the Nebraska tractor tests that the United States soon adopted them as its national standard. Nebraska still tests all new tractors sold in the United States to this day, to ensure adherence to international OECD standards.

Horsepower testing at Nebraska.

150 HP
DYNAMOMETER

USED TO MEASURE PTO HORSEPOWER

$$HP = \frac{POUNDS \times RPM}{3000}$$

What Nebraska Tested in 1949

Test A: "Limber up" test, to help run-in a new tractor and check all is working as it should.

Test B: 100 percent maximum belt power test, measuring horsepower to make sure the engine is thoroughly warm and at full load.

Test C: Maximum belt power at leaner carburetor setting recommended by manufacturer.

Test D: One-hour rated belt test. Fuel consumption measured. If there is no manufacturer's rating, assume it to be 85 percent of the 100 percent maximum belt load test.

Test E: Varying load belt test. Six 20-minute runs: at rated load; no load; max load; one-half torque load; one-quarter torque load; and three-quarter torque load.

Test F: 100 percent maximum drawbar load, measuring horsepower, made in rated gear.

Test G: Operating maximum drawbar load in each forward gear, engine at rated speed.

Test H: Rated load drawbar test, ten hours at rated engine speed in rated gear, fuel consumption measured.

Test I: Drawbar test in rated gear using leaner carburetor setting, and all added weight removed.

Test J: Drawbar test in rated gear using leaner carburetor setting and smaller wheels or tires.

NEBRASKA TESTS

Economy Records—Best and Worst (1920-1984)

- ✓ John Deere 1650 (best diesel) 1983 18.64 hp per hour per gallon
- ✓ Oliver 1800 (best gasoline) 1960 13.18 hp per hour per gallon
- ✓ Farmall M (best distillate) 1939 12.44 hp per hour per gallon
- ✓ Case Model C (best kerosene) 1929 11.36 hp per hour per gallon
- ✓ Case VAC (best tractor fuel) 1949 10.39 hp per hour per gallon
- ✓ Case 910-B (best propane) 1959 9.99 hp per hour per gallon
- ✓ Case 610 (worst diesel) 1959 9.29 hp per hour per gallon
- ✓ Minneapolis-Moline U (worst tractor fuel) 1954 8.68 hp per hour per gallon
- ✓ Ford 640-L (worst propane) 1957 7.26 hp per hour per gallon
- ✓ Fordson All-Around (worst distillate) 1937 6.71 hp per hour per gallon
- ✓ Uncle Sam 20-30 (worst kerosene) 1920 4.85 hp per hour per gallon
- ✓ Shaw Du-All T-25 (worst gasoline) 1927 3.3 hp per hour per gallon

Tractor jam—rush hour at Nebraska.

"GRANDPA GOT RUN OVER BY A JOHN DEERE TRACTOR"

Artist: Cledus T. Judd
Album: Cledus T. Judd
What's the Story?
A parody of the comic song "Grandma Got Run Over by a Reindeer," this tune has an inebriated Grandpa getting hit by a tractor.

THE MOST TRACTORS IN ONE PLACE

The world record for the largest number of tractors working simultaneously has been broken many times. What is it about the Australians, South Africans, English, and Irish? They must love their tractors.

Number of tractors working simultaneously:

107	South Africa (April 10, 1999)
299	New South Wales, Australia (April 15, 2001)
730	South Africa (April 20, 2002)
1,802	County Louth, Ireland (August 6, 2002)
1,897	New South Wales, Australia (April 12, 2004)
2,141	Wiltshire, England (June 25, 2006)
4,752	County Louth, Ireland (August 5, 2007)

Threshing

The threshing (formerly called "thrashing") machine was invented by Scottish engineer Andrew Meikle around 1784. It separated grain from husk mechanically, far faster than with the traditional method of hand flailing. The machines were popular with farmers, but not with the laborers whose livelihoods were threatened; as a result, southern England saw widespread riots in 1830. First powered by steam traction engines via a belt, threshing machines were increasingly powered by tractors from the 1920s onward. Allis-Chalmers's heavyweight Model A was designed specifically for this job. But the coming of the self-propelled combine spelled the end of the thresher, and after World War II their use rapidly dropped off.

CHARLES PARR & CHARLES HART
Most Important Tractor: HART-PARR 12-25

Most of the early American tractor makers, like John Deere or J. I. Case, were long established in the agricultural machinery business. Hart-Parr was quite different. Charles Parr and Charles Hart were engineering students at the University of Wisconsin, who began designing and making engines while they were still in college.

College Friends with a Big Idea
Immediately after graduation in 1896, they formed a company to build stationary engines, and by all accounts they did well, soon outgrowing their first workshop and moving to Charles City, Iowa, in order to expand. By 1900, it was clear that farm tractors were a new and expanding market, and the two

Charleses built their first in 1902, powered by one of their own twin-cylinder 30 hp units. The engine also had oil cooling, to which Hart-Parr stayed faithful well into the 1920s—oil would not freeze, and it allowed higher, more-efficient running temperatures than water cooling would.

Early Hart-Parr tractors were massive machines, distinctive with their large rectangular cooling tower at the front. Designed for the big prairie farms of the US and Canada, they were used for plowing and heavy haulage as well as powering threshers. The biggest Hart-Parr 60-100 tractor weighed 29.2 tons (26.5 tonnes).

PRE-POWER STEERING

Before the days of factory-installed power steering, farmers needed big biceps in order to steer their tractors, especially when making low-speed headland turns or maneuvering in the yard. The University of Nebraska testers devised a mechanism to measure steering effort, and in 1952 an aftermarket power-steering system was offered in the United States.

For $180/£109 (approximately $1,465/£890 today), buyers got a complete kit, including an hydraulic pump (powered by the engine), an hydraulic motor coupled to the steering wheel shaft, and all the necessary hoses and fittings—they just had to install it themselves.

Early power steering? No, a device to measure steering effort.

TOP TIPS
Do not drive close to the edge of a ditch!

THE TRACTOR EXPLOSION

Number of tractor companies, tractors produced, and horses or mules on US farms, 1904-1920

YEAR	TRACTOR COMPANIES	TRACTOR PRODUCTION	HORSES/MULES (MILLIONS)
1904	6	-	19.5
1905	6	-	20.0
1906	9	-	22.1
1907	8	-	23.5
1908	6	-	23.9
1909	9	2000	24.7
1910	15	4000	25.1
1911	20	7000	24.6
1912	31	11,500	24.9
1913	39	7000	25.0
1914	58	15,000	25.4
1915	61	21,000	25.7
1916	114	29,670	25.8
1917	124	62,742	25.9
1918	142	132,697	26.4
1919	164	164,590	26.4
1920	166	203,207	26.1

(Source: Farm Machinery and Equipment, 15 Sept 1937)

WHY BALLAST?

Why do farmers put balance weights on tractors? If they're so worried about fuel consumption and costs, why would they haul around all that extra weight?

They do this to control wheel slip. Wheel slip is best seen as a sort of safety valve for the tractor's massive torque. If the wheels weren't allowed to slip by a certain amount, then all of the tractor's torque would force its way through the transmission, wearing out the drivetrain prematurely. Of course, too much wheel slip will wear out the tires early—a situation that is not quite as serious as transmission failure but is still not cheap—so farmers need to strike a balance between transmission and tire wear in addition to monitoring fuel economy.

It came from outer space...or it could have been an experimental clover harvester. One of the two.

Torque Amplifier

This was International Harvester's take on the new thing for tractors in the 1950s—a two-range transmission with power shifting between the two ranges. Commonly known as the "TA," International Harvester's version was a planetary gear unit located in the clutch housing that doubled the tractor's forward speeds to ten, with two reverse ratios. Soon, other manufacturers rushed to follow International Harvester's lead—Minneapolis-Moline's version was named "Ampli-Torq," but it did exactly the same job.

Diesel-Electric Tractor

Diesel-electric power units are more often associated with railway locomotives, but in 1999, German machinery dealer Schmetz built a working diesel-electric tractor. Based on a New Holland M135, the Eltrac 135 used the standard diesel engine to drive a generator, which in turn powered a water-cooled electric motor.

Several advantages were claimed. The motor allowed for a smooth, stepless transmission, like that of a CVT but far simpler mechanically. Electric motors give full power from a standing start, so the Eltrac could accelerate more rapidly than a conventional tractor. Journalists were impressed by this, and also by the fact that the motor was strong enough to pull a four-furrow plow with ease.

A Versatile Machine

The Eltrac could also power electric-trailed machinery and even act as a stand-alone generator in the event of a power loss. As with any diesel-electric, it also allowed the engine to run at a more constant and efficient speed. Schmetz thought that the Eltrac would cost around $1,650/£1,000 (approximately $2,136/£1,296 today) more than an equivalent conventional tractor, but that its advantages made this amount well worthwhile.

Nothing more was heard of the Eltrac, but the idea of a diesel-electric tractor still makes a lot of sense.

Fuel Cell Tractor

In the twenty-first century, everyone is talking about fuel cells, usually hydrogen powered, as the future of private transportation when oil runs out. Well, the fuel cell idea is nothing new—Allis-Chalmers built a working fuel-cell tractor back in 1959.

Based on an Allis D12, this used a great block of 1,008 fuel cells, which together produced 15 kW, powering a 20 hp DC electric motor. According to Allis-Chalmer's publicity department, that was enough to pull a two-furrow plow. The tractor was also very simple to operate—it had no gears, of course, and just one lever to control forward speed.

But the world's enthusiasm for fuel cells seems to come in waves, and as this receded, so did the Allis-Chalmers fuel-cell tractor.

GEARS ARE POWER HOGS

Tractor transmissions, even the latest electronically controlled systems, are not very efficient. The majority, 75 to 85 percent, of engine power is lost on its way to the wheels.

Looks good, but it's not that efficient.

Bread-Making Tractor

H. P. Saunderson, an English tractor pioneer, dreamt up an ingenious publicity stunt for his Saunderson Universal in 1906. He decided that it would make bread before the eyes of a crowd of gathered journalists.

A Universal pulled two binders to harvest 2 acres (0.8 hectares) of wheat. Then the binder was unhitched, and the tractor carried the sheaves to a threshing machine. The Universal's belt pulley then powered the thresher, and then a grinder, turning the harvested grain into flour.

A baker took over, turning the flour into dough and baking loaves of bread. Meanwhile, the tractor was set to work plowing the recently harvested 2 acres

(0.8 hectares), cultivating it, and sowing seed for the next crop of wheat, all while the journalists looked on. In five hours, the tractor had harvested, threshed, and ground one crop and sown the next one, while the journalists were able to munch on the freshly baked bread the tractor had helped produce. It was a fine way to demonstrate the adaptability of a good tractor.

Correct weight distribution is essential for efficient working.

CORRECT WEIGHT DISTRIBUTION

The ideal front-rear weight distribution varies according to the job at hand and type of tractor:

Tractor type	Weight distribution: Front percentage	Rear percentage
Two-wheel drive	25–35	75–65
MFWD	35–40	65–60
4WD (towed implements)	51–55	49–45
4WD (hitched implements)	55–60	45–40

Early History Of Tractor Pulling

Tractor pulling is a worldwide sport, and a very simple one. The idea is to see how far a tractor can haul a heavily ballasted sled along a 328-foot (100 m) track—the farther they get, the heavier the load, as the sled transfers its weight from rear to front.

Back in the early twentieth century, American farmers were competing in horse-pulling contests to see who had the strongest plowing horse. The first recorded tractor pulls took place in Vaughnsville, Ohio, and Bowling Green, Missouri, in 1929. Back then, the measurements were crude— standard tractors had to pull a heavily loaded skidpan over 10 yards (9.1 m), and the winner was often the one tractor that didn't break in half!

FENDT VARIO

DATES: FROM 1995

WHY IS IT IMPORTANT? FIRST HIGH-POWER TRACTOR WITH FULLY AUTOMATIC TRANSMISSION.

ENGINE TYPE: WATER-COOLED, SIX-CYLINDER, 423 CI (6.9 L)

POWER: 260 HP

WEIGHT: 18,040 POUNDS (8,200 KG)

PRICE: $175,508/£106,700 (APPROXIMATELY $248,397/£150,998 TODAY)

GOOD POINTS: AUTO TRANSMISSION KEEPS ENGINE AT OPTIMUM SPEED.

BAD POINTS: NONE YET.

RANDOM FACT: FENDT'S VARIO 900 IS THE MOST POWERFUL AUTOMATIC TRANSMISSION TRACTOR IN THE WORLD.

HISTORY: If design trends carry on as they are now, then the Fendt Vario's CVT system will be the tractor transmission of the future, certainly for medium and high horsepower. The CVT is a fully automatic setup, using a combination of mechanical and hydrostatic systems to give infinitely variable ratios from 6 to 31 mph (10 to 50 kph).

In the past, a mechanical "step-less" transmission would have been very complex, and a hydrostatic would have been too inefficient. The Fendt Vario uses elements of both, and it claims to combine the best of both worlds. By all accounts, it works very well, giving a smooth transition from zero miles per hour to top speed, and eliminating the need for any gear changes. In the field, the transmission automatically shifts ratios to keep the engine at its optimum speed. On the Fendt, the transmission's electronics are integrated with those of the engine, so that the two components work together.

Fendt's gamble paid off, and the Vario sold well. In fact, it sold so well that the company extended the CVT option downward into the rest of its tractor line and sold the transmission to other tractor manufacturers. No doubt about it, the step-less transmission is a big step forward.

WHAT, NO GEARS? TRUE, BUT THE FENDT VARIO HAS AN
INFINITE NUMBER OF RATIOS.

An Intelligent Tractor

Back in 1996, the Silsoe Research Institute developed a driverless tractor that could not only steer itself but also tell the difference between a crop plant and a weed! The "tractor" (really a frame on wheels, and of course having no driver it didn't need a cab) had a camera mounted at the front that enabled it to "see" about fifteen plants in front. It was programmed to look for three straight rows, and the images were compared with standard pictures of the crop, weeds and soil.

Once it determined whether a plant was crop or weed, the tractor's computer would turn the herbicide spray on or off, as needed. The tractor was steered by means of steering angle sensors and a compass (GPS was not yet available, of course), and when the camera detected no plants at all, the tractor made a headland turn and headed back across the field.

Who's driving this thing?

JOHN DEERE'S BIG GAMBLE

For over forty years, John Deere stayed faithful to the chuggy twin-cylinder layout they'd started out with. All around them, rivals went to four cylinders, but Johnny Popper kept on popping along.

By the mid-1950s, it was clear that radical change was needed, as the power limitations of a mere two cylinders became increasingly obvious. So John Deere, never one of the industry's innovators, took the bold step of replacing its entire range in one go. In great secrecy, a design team got down to developing a completely new lineup of three- and four-cylinder Deeres that would finally consign Johnny Popper to history.

Seven years later, in August 1960, the new line was unveiled in Dallas in a lavish launch ceremony. Press and public loved them, and despite being 95 percent new, the new machines had no mechanical disasters, recalls, or redesigns. John Deere's gamble had paid off.

TRY, TRY AGAIN

As the tractor developed, manufacturers tried just about every combination of wheel type, size, and construction.

An illustration from the early twentieth century shows a bewildering choice of wheel, drum, and track arrangements. Everything from a conventional four-wheel, two-wheel-drive front-steering tractor, to a full crawler. Everything else in between makes its own interpretation of the ideal layout for a tractor. And every one of these layouts was tried.

DIESEL WINS OUT

Fuel type used by tractors tested at University of Nebraska

Year	Gasoline*	Distillate*	LPG*	Diesel*
1949	60	14	5	23
1950	65	8	0	25
1955	55	5	8	35
1960	35	0	20	45
1965	38	0	8	50
1970	34	0	0	66
1975	8	0	0	92
1979	0	0	0	100

*Numbers given indicate percent of tractors using each type of fuel.

SWEDISH CAR-BASED TRACTORS

The Model T conversions faded away, but car-based tractors surfaced again in Sweden during World War II, when a shortage of tractors led to a new rash of conversions. They were termed "EPA" tractors, which wasn't a term of admiration—EPA was a chain of low-quality discount stores.

The conversion, from car or truck to tractor, was very simple. The rear passenger space was cut out and two gearboxes installed in a row, to gear down to tractor speeds and allow the EPA to haul heavy trailers.

After the war, EPAs survived in Sweden, and spread to other countries, though not always working as tractors. Still classed as tractors, they could often be legally driven by teenagers too young to have a car license. In 1975, Swedish legislators closed this loophole with a new category A tractor, still an EPA conversion, but with a top speed of 18 mph (29 kph).

Electric Soviet Tractors

In Soviet Russia of the 1930s to 1950s, engineers were fascinated by the concept of the electric tractor. But they didn't use battery power—just very long cables! Mobile transformers were wheeled into the field, and tapped into overhead power lines. The tractor (whether a wheeled or crawler machine) carried an immensely long cable on a drum, which delivered the power where it was needed.

It sounds impractical, but an XTZ-12 electric crawler, built at the Kharkov works in 1954, was claimed to work 450 acres (182 hectares) without having to move its power source. The crawler carried its power cable high, strung over the back so as not to interfere with the plow. The Soviets built electric combine harvesters as well, which were said to be able to cover 550 acres (222 hectares) without moving the substation. An electric sugar beet harvester used a cable that was 0.62 mile (1 km) long.

Index

Credits

Quarto would like to thank the following for kindly supplying images for inclusion in this book:

AGCO Corporation/FENDT 15t, 20, 32t, 34, 57bl, 65b, 80, 83t, 90, 93t, 136t, 148, 152, 183
Dover: 21bl
Peter Henshaw 14tl, 17t, 26r, 29, 30–31, 44–45, 46b, 53, 54t, 55tr, 62t, 67, 85, 91, 99, 115t, 127t, 129, 138–139, 140, 145, 156, 176
Istock
John Deere 10–11, 12b, 18–19, 21t, 22–23, 37, 38t, 39t, 49, 52, 64, 73b, 82t, 87, 99, 100t, 111mr, 119b, 129b, 132–133, 134–135, 137, 141, 147, 149, 150b, 170t
JCB 33, 40mr, 88t, 109, 143, 185
Andrew Morland 13, 16r, 25, 28, 37, 41b, 42b, 51, 55b, 61, 67t, 70–71, 79r, 89t, 95, 96, 105, 107, 110t, 113, 167b, 169
Nebraska Tractor Museum 12t, 14b, 35, 40t, 42bl, 46t, 56t, 58, 63, 75, 77, 78, 82b, 101t, 114, 122t, 123b, 125, 126mr, 130t, 137, 146, 153t, 157b, 159, 160–161, 163, 172–173, 174–175, 177, 178
Profi 16t, 68
The Agricultural Tractor 1855–1950 (1954 USDA Publication) www.asabe.org: 21r, 26r, 33t, 69b, 85, 157t
Trantor: 108

Author's Acknowledgments

All sorts of people helped me compile this book, and it wouldn't have happened without them. So hats off to photographer Andrew Morland, to Mary Ellen Ducey of the University of Nebraska, and to staff at Kingston Maurward Agricultural College. To the press officers of Massey-Ferguson, CNH Global, John Deere, Fendt, JCB, Trantor, and New Holland Basildon. Also to Martin Richards and the Bartlett, Barlow, and Davis families, not to mention all the other tractor owners and collectors whose machines appear in this book.

Thank you, one and all.

Peter Henshaw
Sherborne, England,
October 2009

The Nebraska Tractor Test Lab and Larsen Tractor Museum

Nebraska is known around the world for testing tractor performance. The Nebraska Tractor Test Law, passed in 1919, has encouraged the manufacture of high quality and reliable tractors for over 90 years. Today the results of Nebraska Tests are made available to the public providing data in five performance areas: power-take-off horsepower, drawbar horsepower, three-point lift capacity, hydraulic flow, and sound levels. This data is available through the Nebraska Tractor Test Laboratory, http://tractortestlab.unl.edu.

The history of the Nebraska Test is preserved within the original tractor test laboratory serving today as the University of Nebraska-Lincoln Larsen Tractor Museum. This museum is named for former Nebraska Test Engineer Lester F. Larsen. He was instrumental in initiating the collection of historic tractor test equipment, as well as acquiring tractors that illustrate key developments in agricultural mechanization over the decades. Visitors are welcome to tour the museum and the modern tractor test lab, both located on the University of Nebraska-Lincoln East Campus. For more information, visit http://tractormuseum.unl.edu.

The Larsen Museum has a mission to be the premier steward of advancements in agricultural technology through the development of collections, exhibits, and programs for public benefit. Collections becoming available online for the public include historic photographs, tractor test reports, tractor advertising literature, and manuals for tractor operation, maintenance and repair. The Larsen Tractor Museum Collections is available through the University of Nebraska-Lincoln Digital Collections, http://contentdm.unl.edu/.

Larsen Tractor Museum
35th and Fair Streets
P.O. Box 830833
Lincoln, NE 68583, 402-472-8389
TractorMuseumArchives@unl.edu

Nebraska Tractor Test Lab
35th & East Campus Loup
P.O. Box 830832
Lincoln, NE 68583, 402-472-2442
tractortestlab@unl.edu